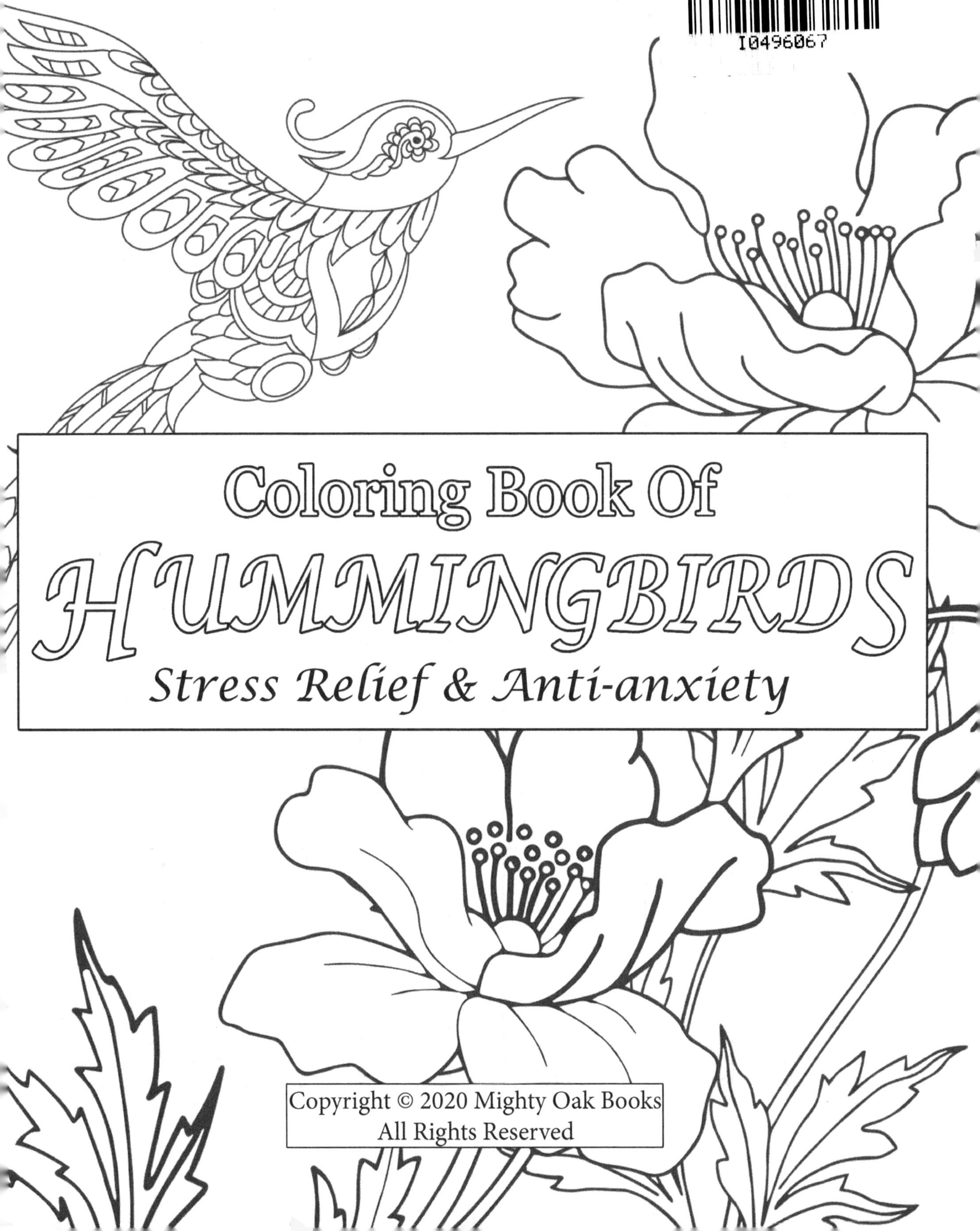

Coloring Book Of HUMMINGBIRDS

Stress Relief & Anti-anxiety

Color Test Page

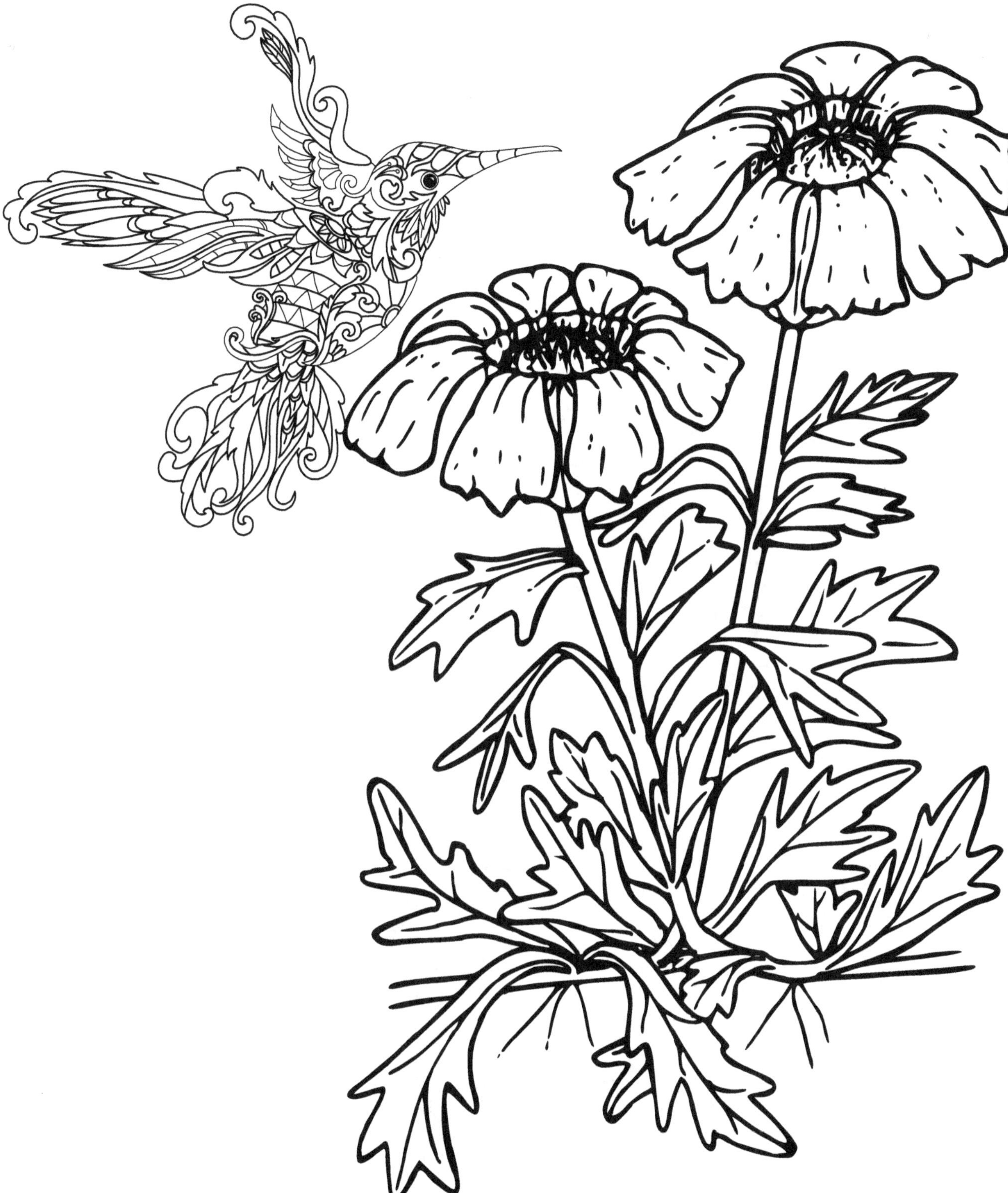

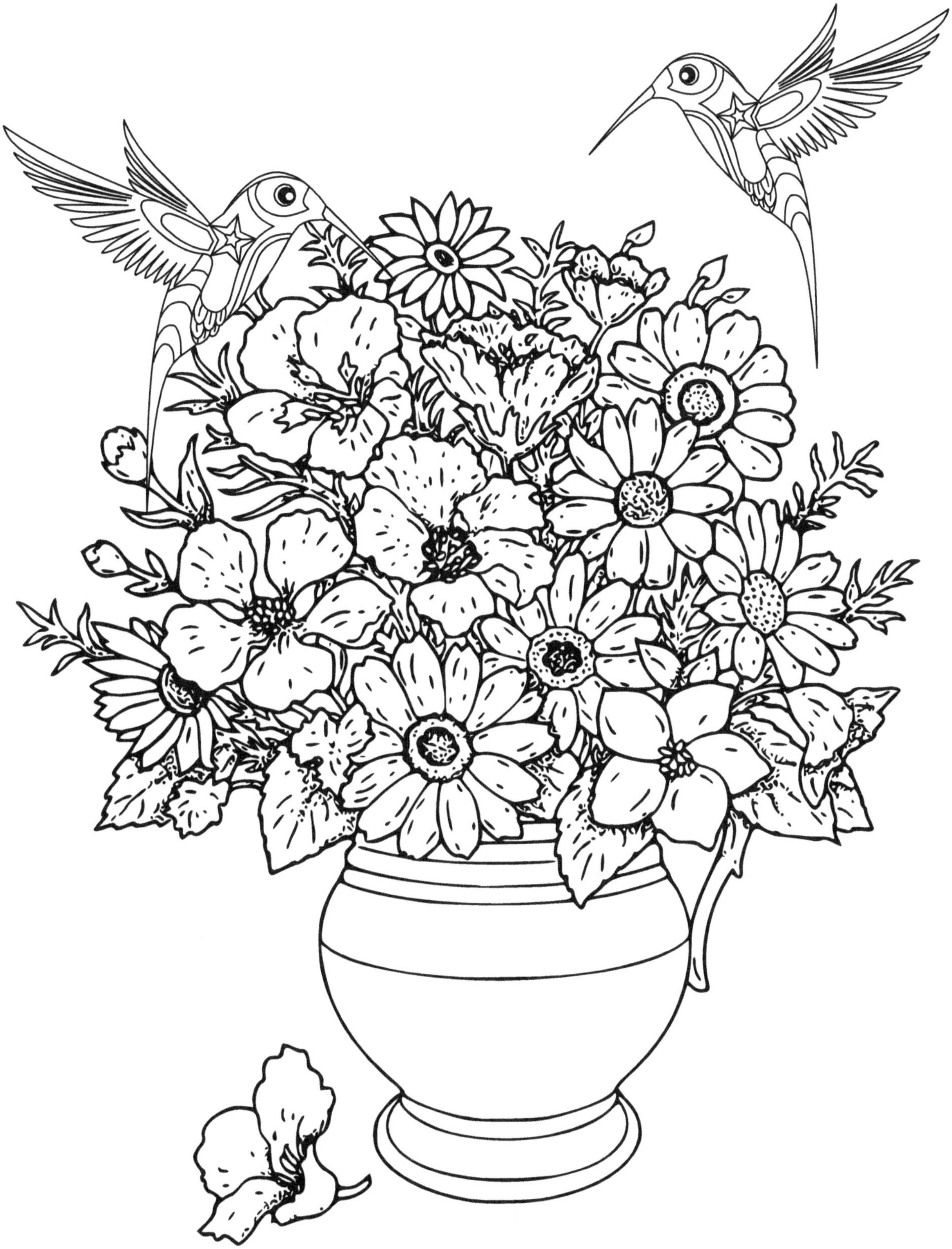

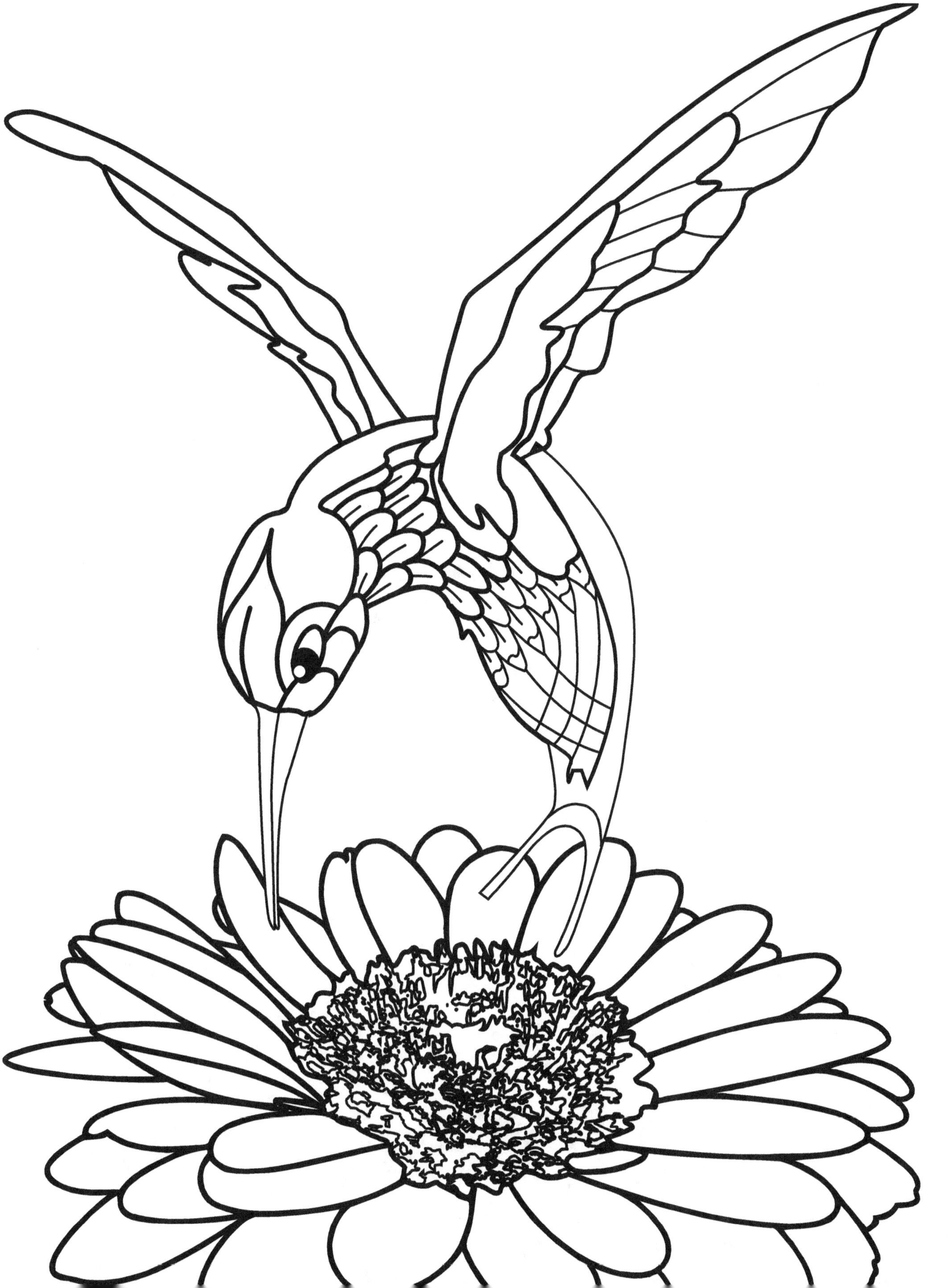

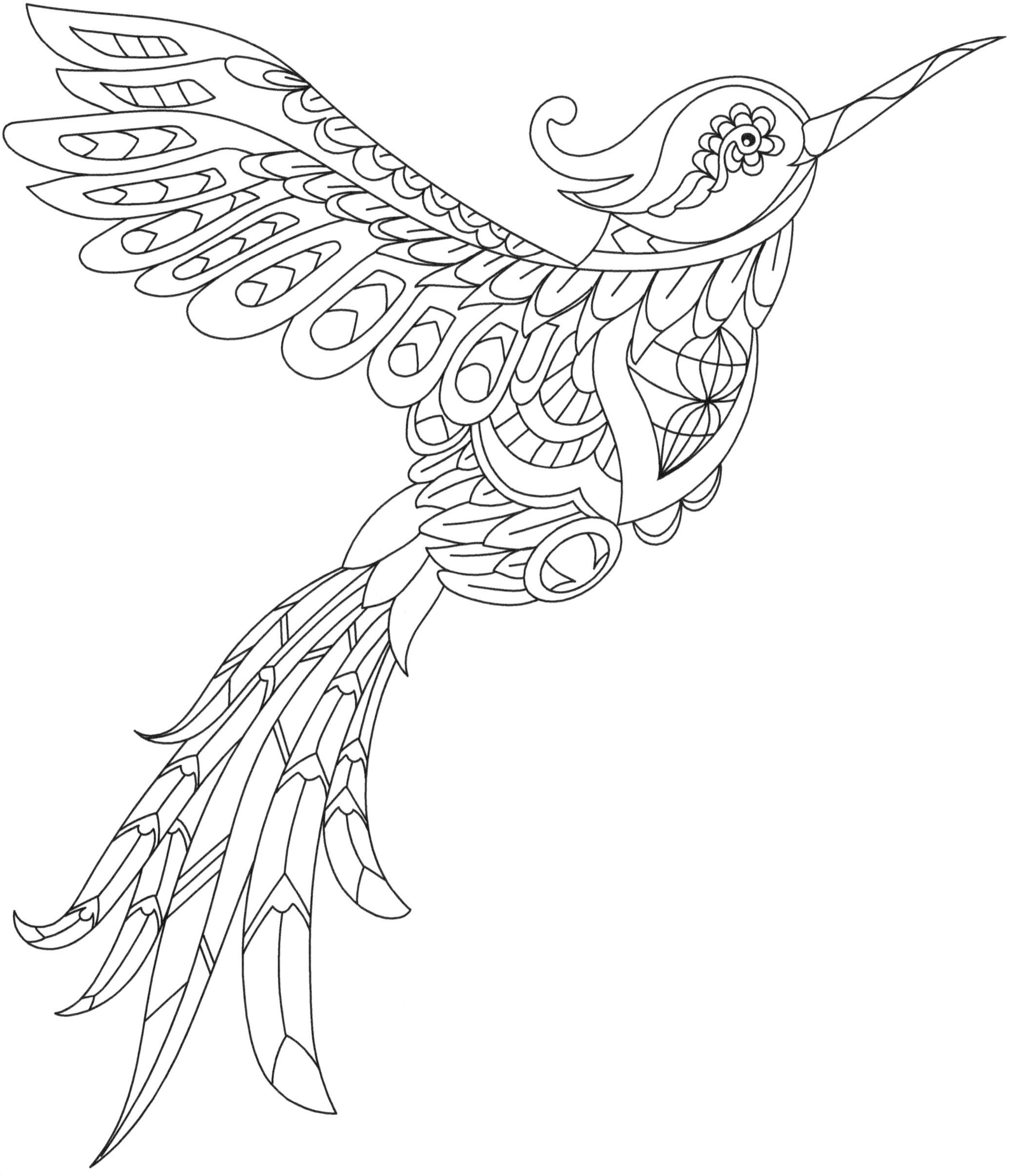

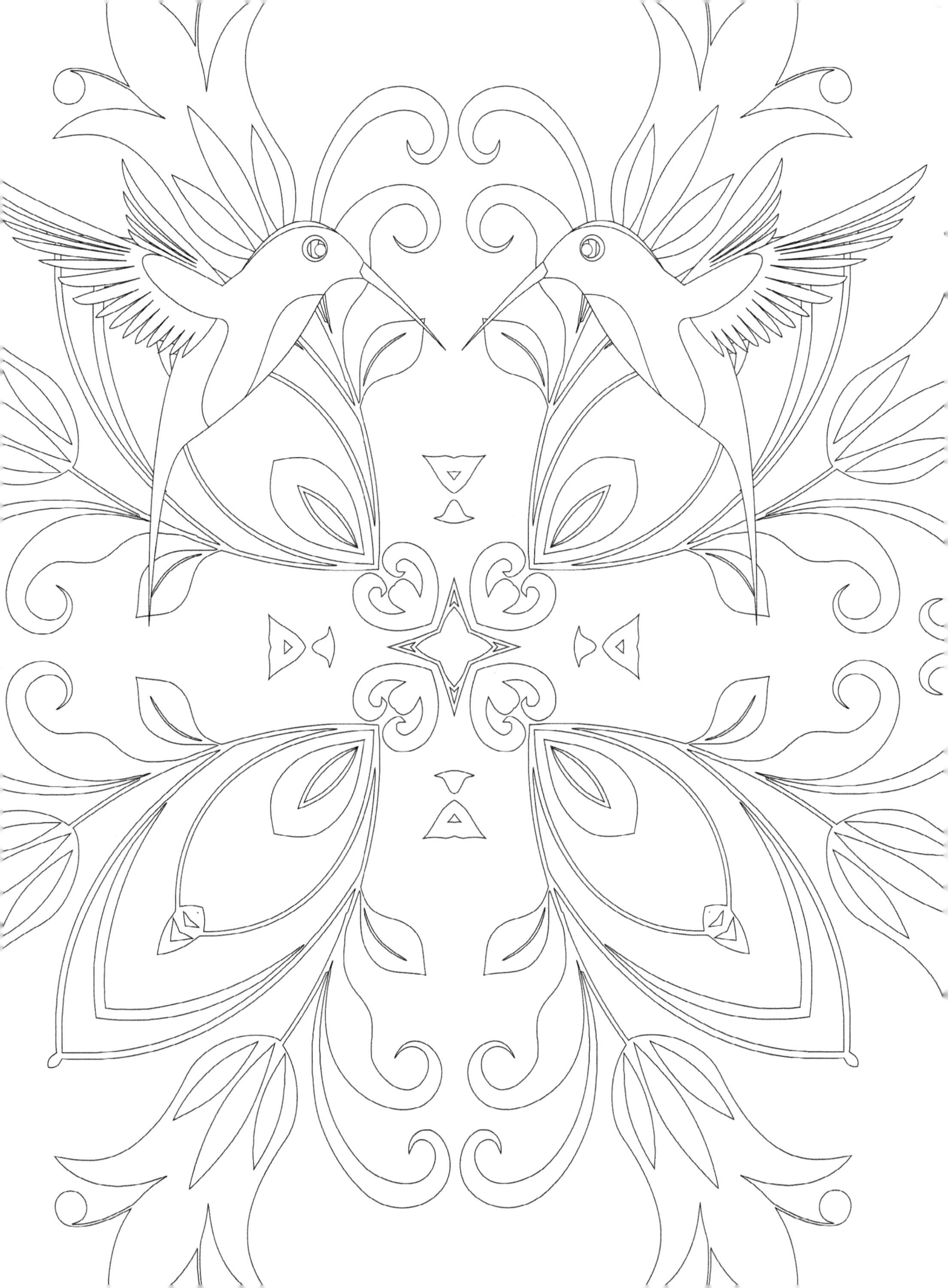

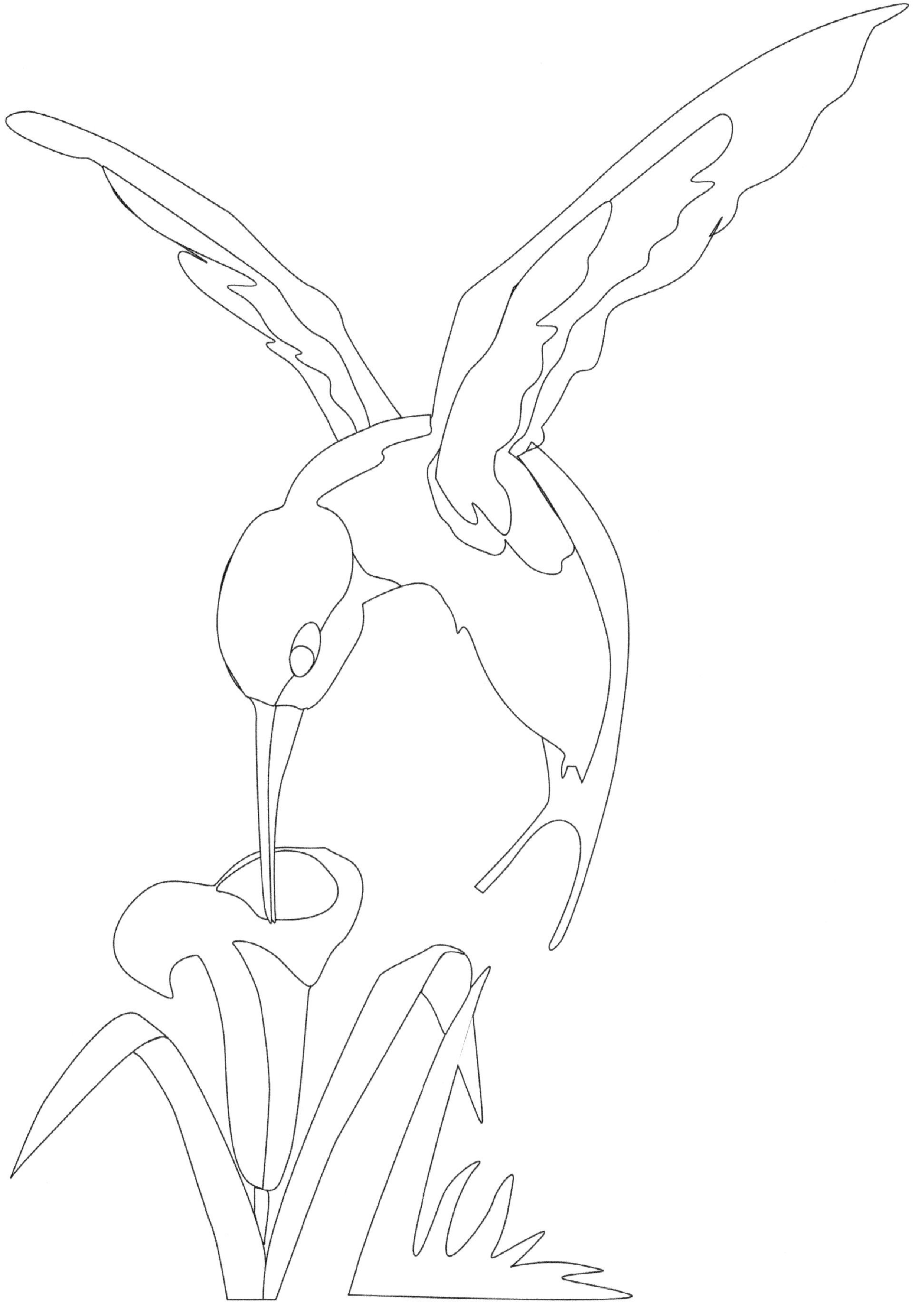

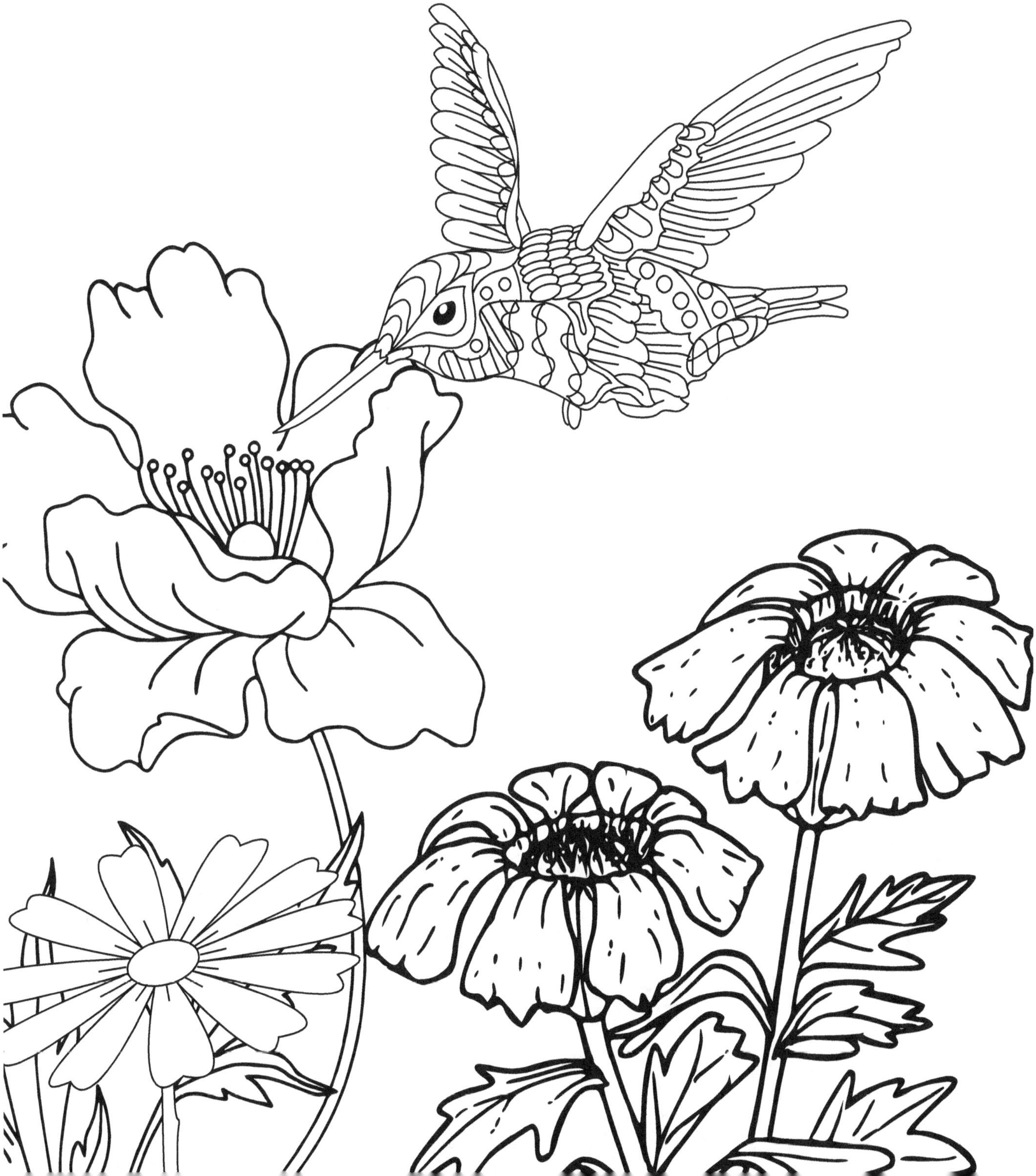

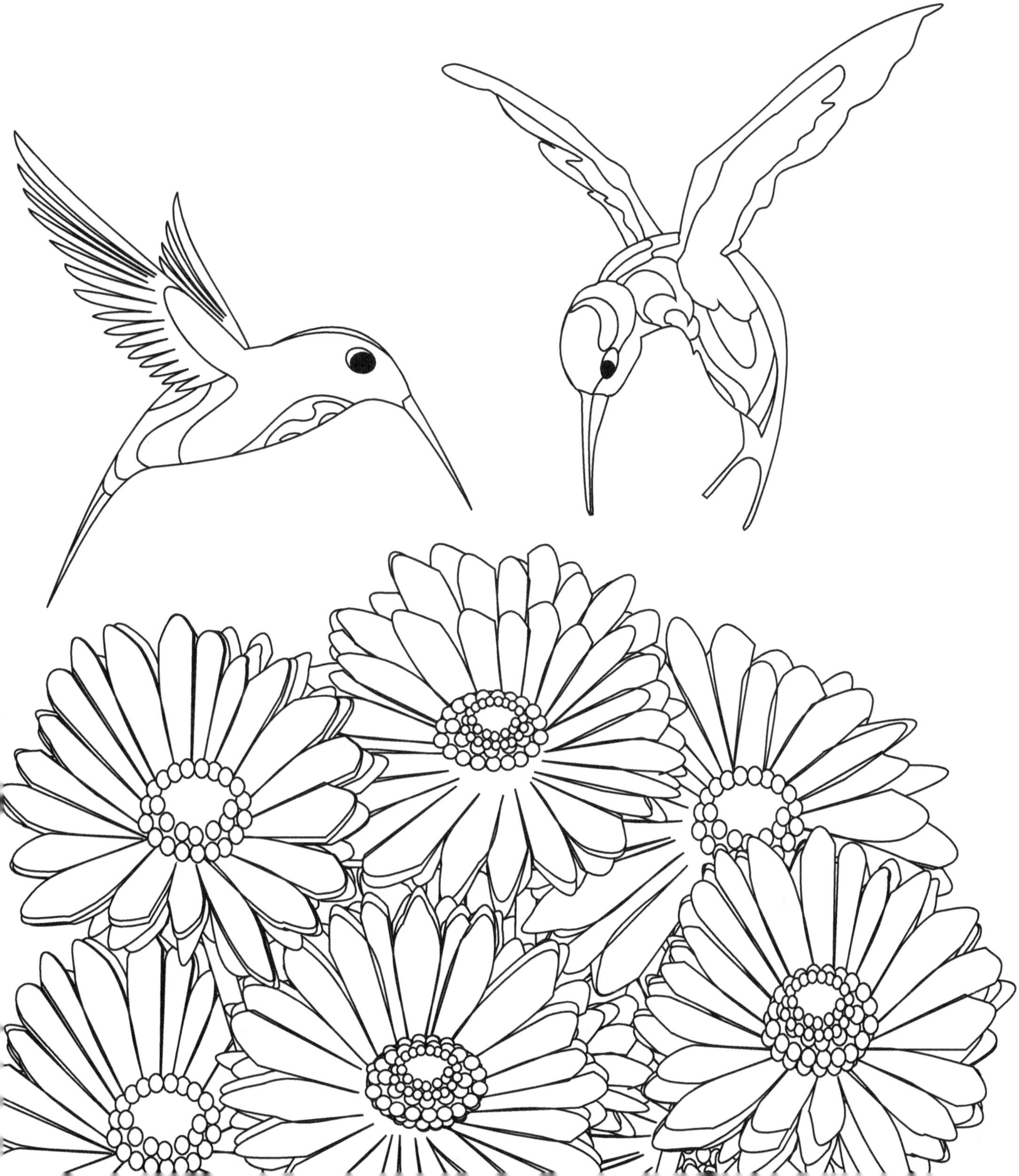

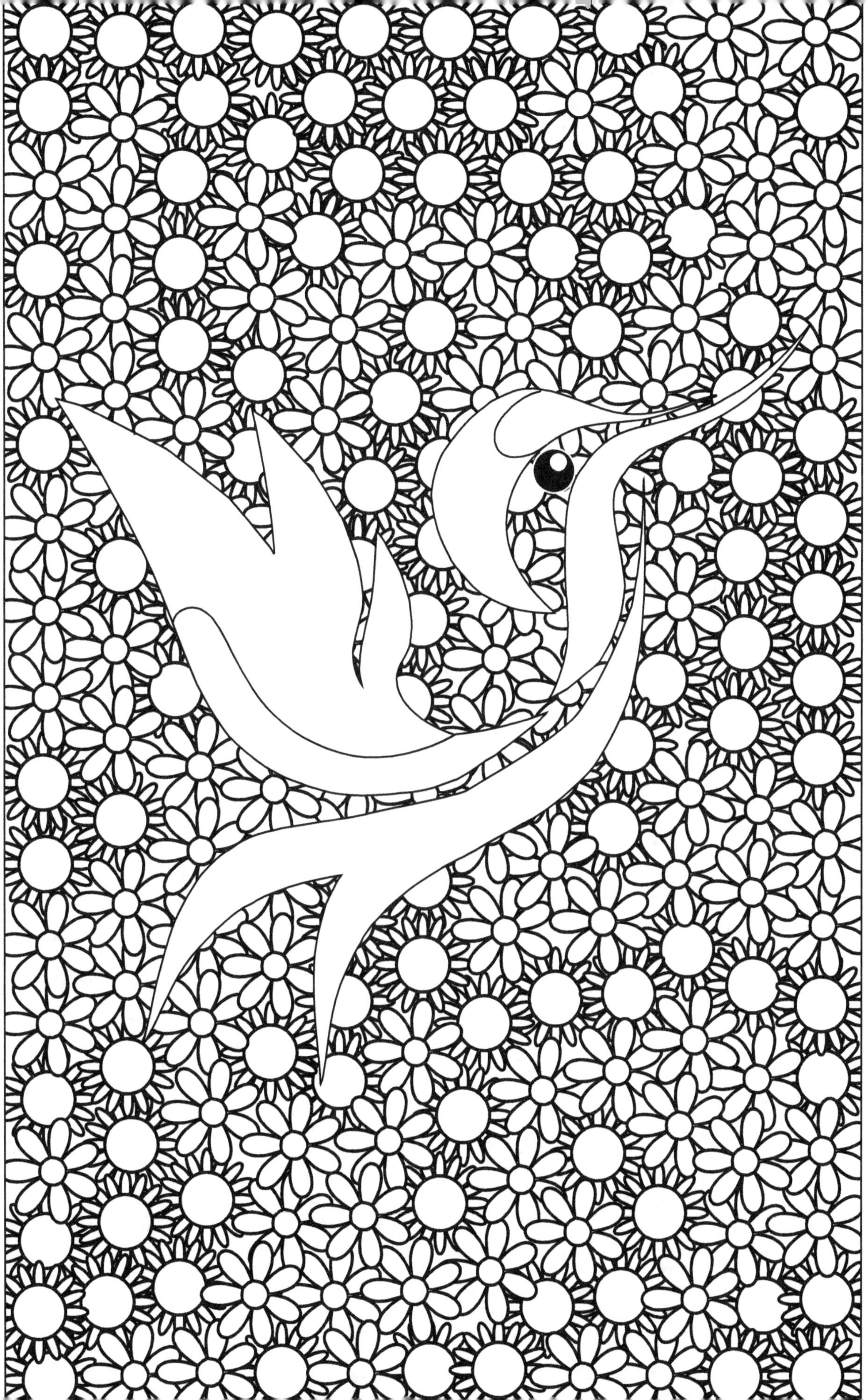

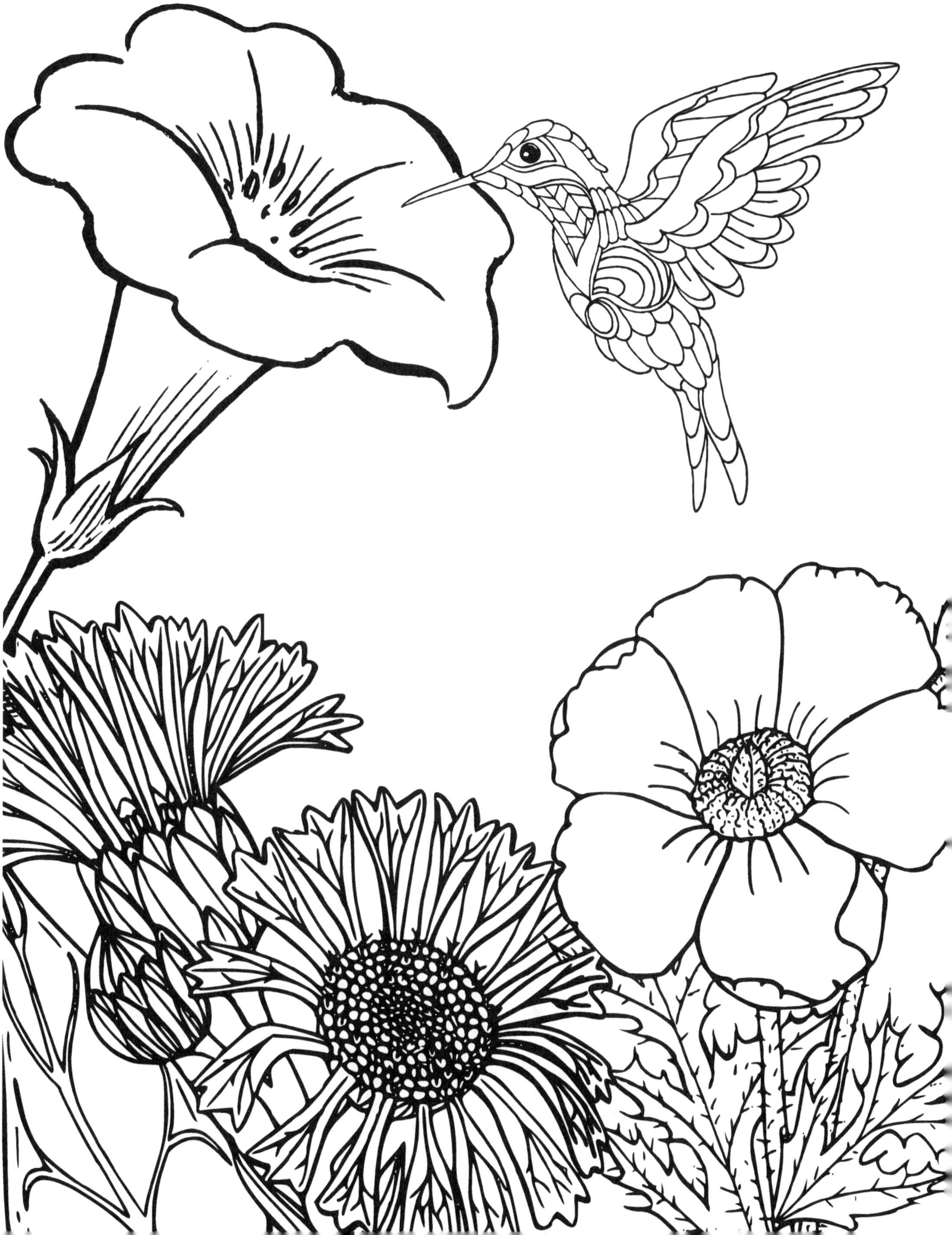

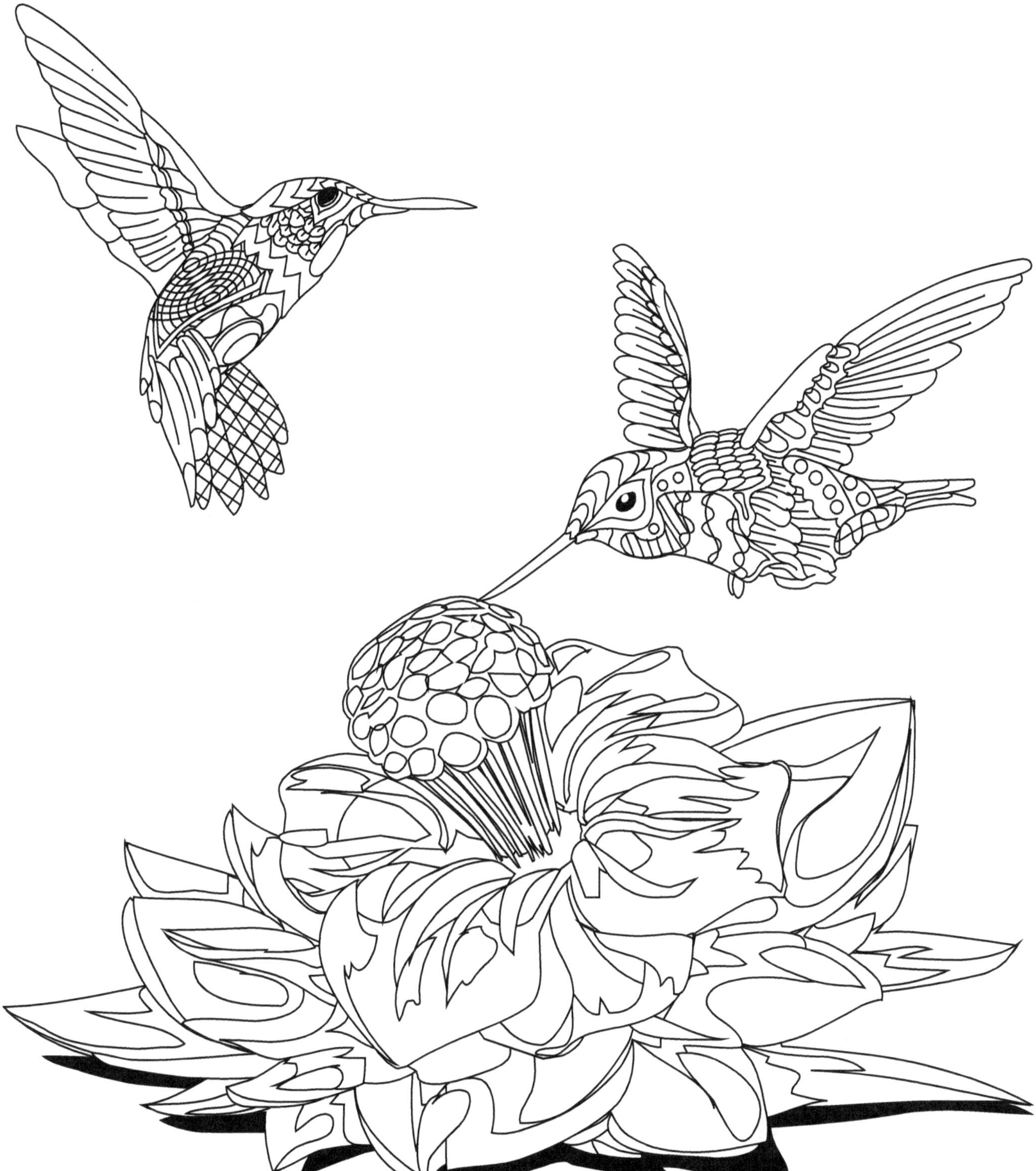

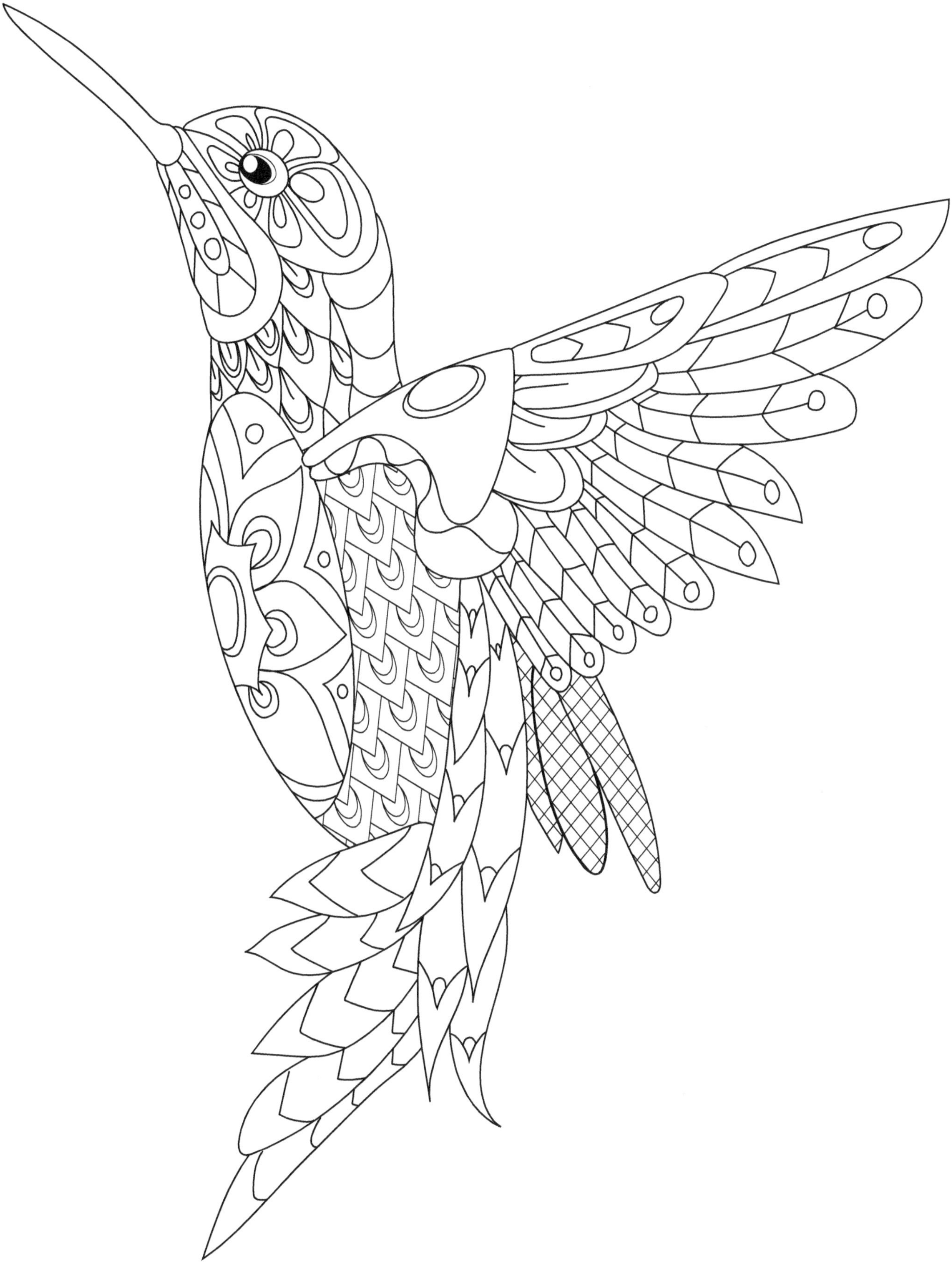

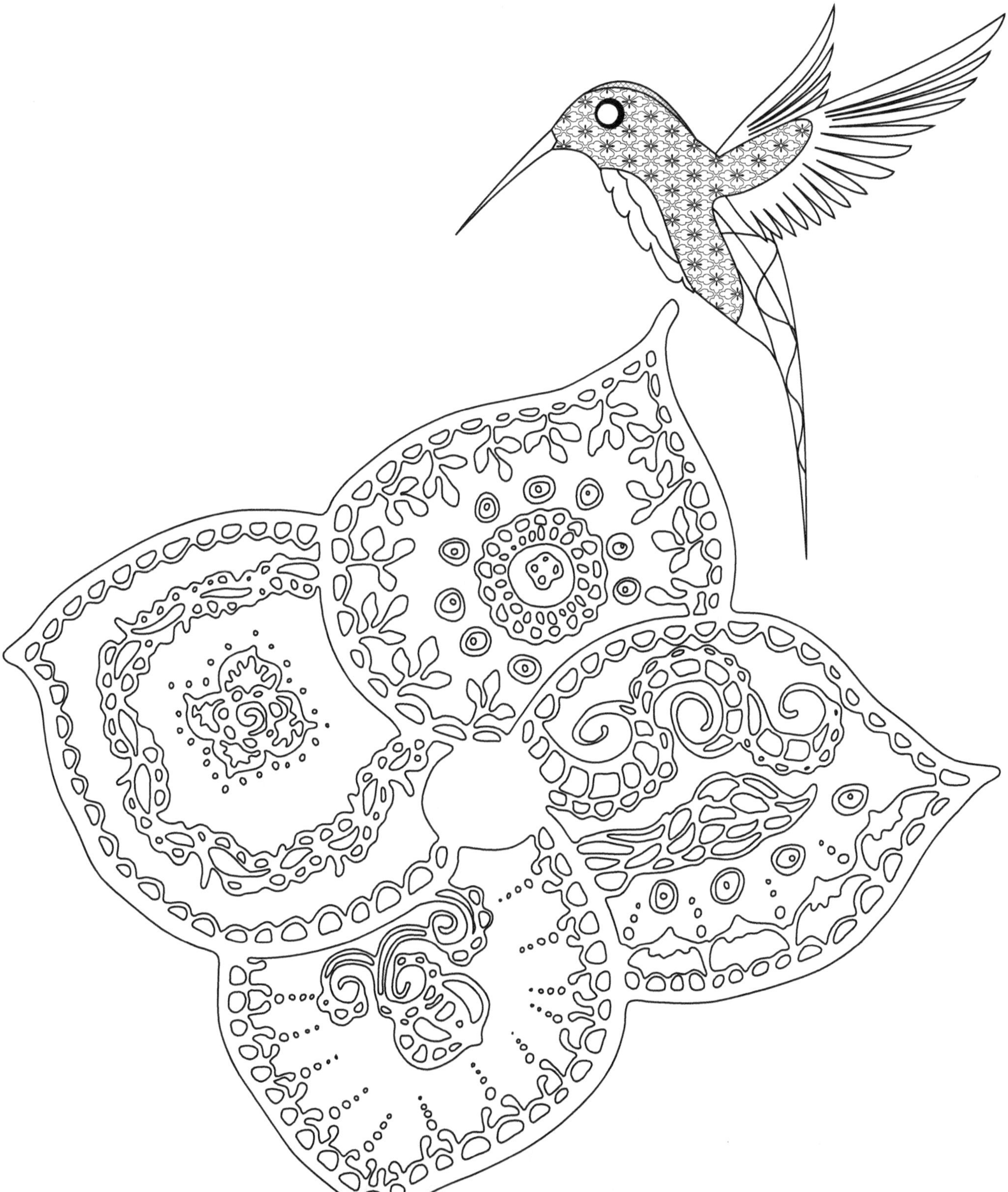

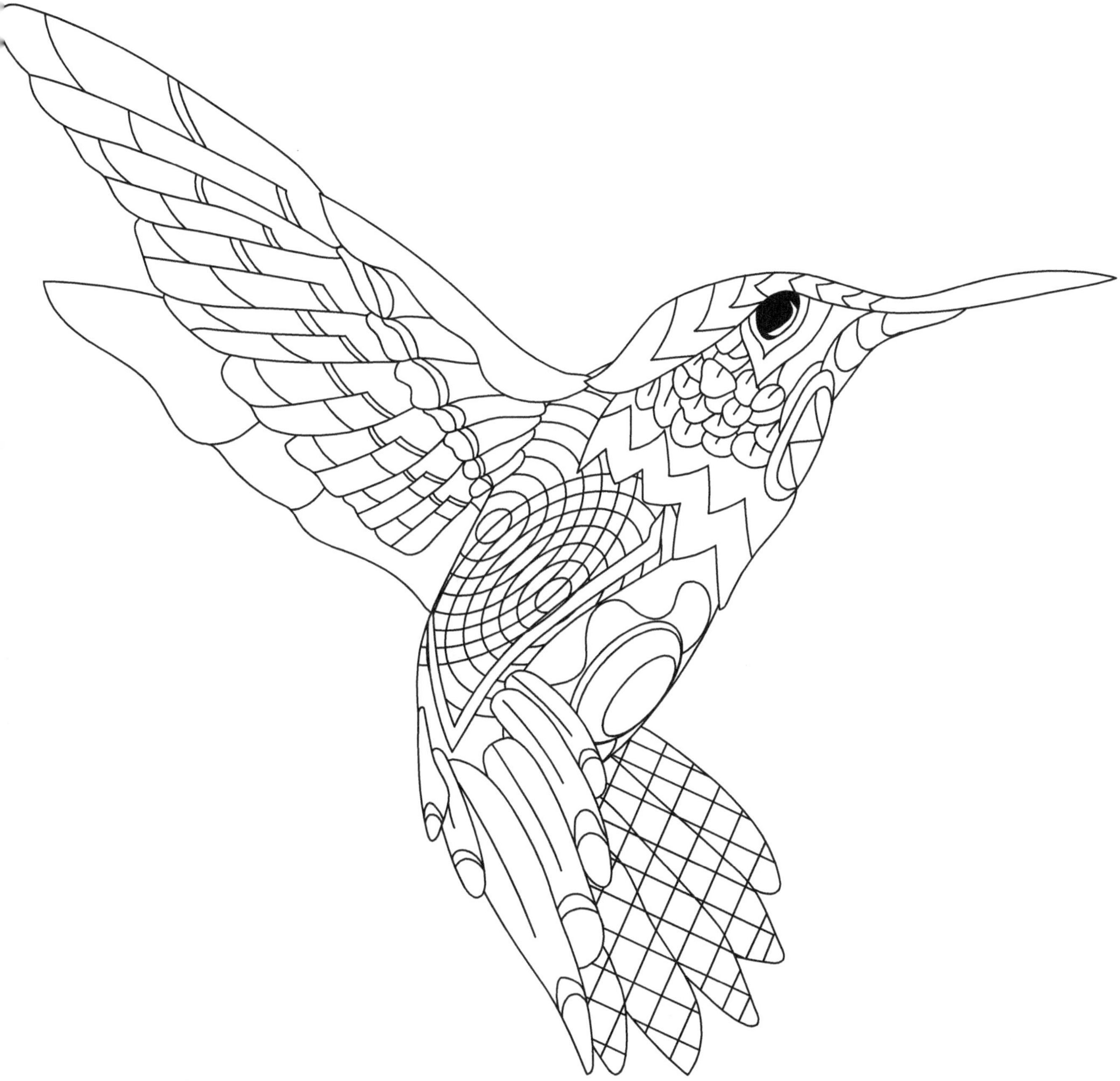

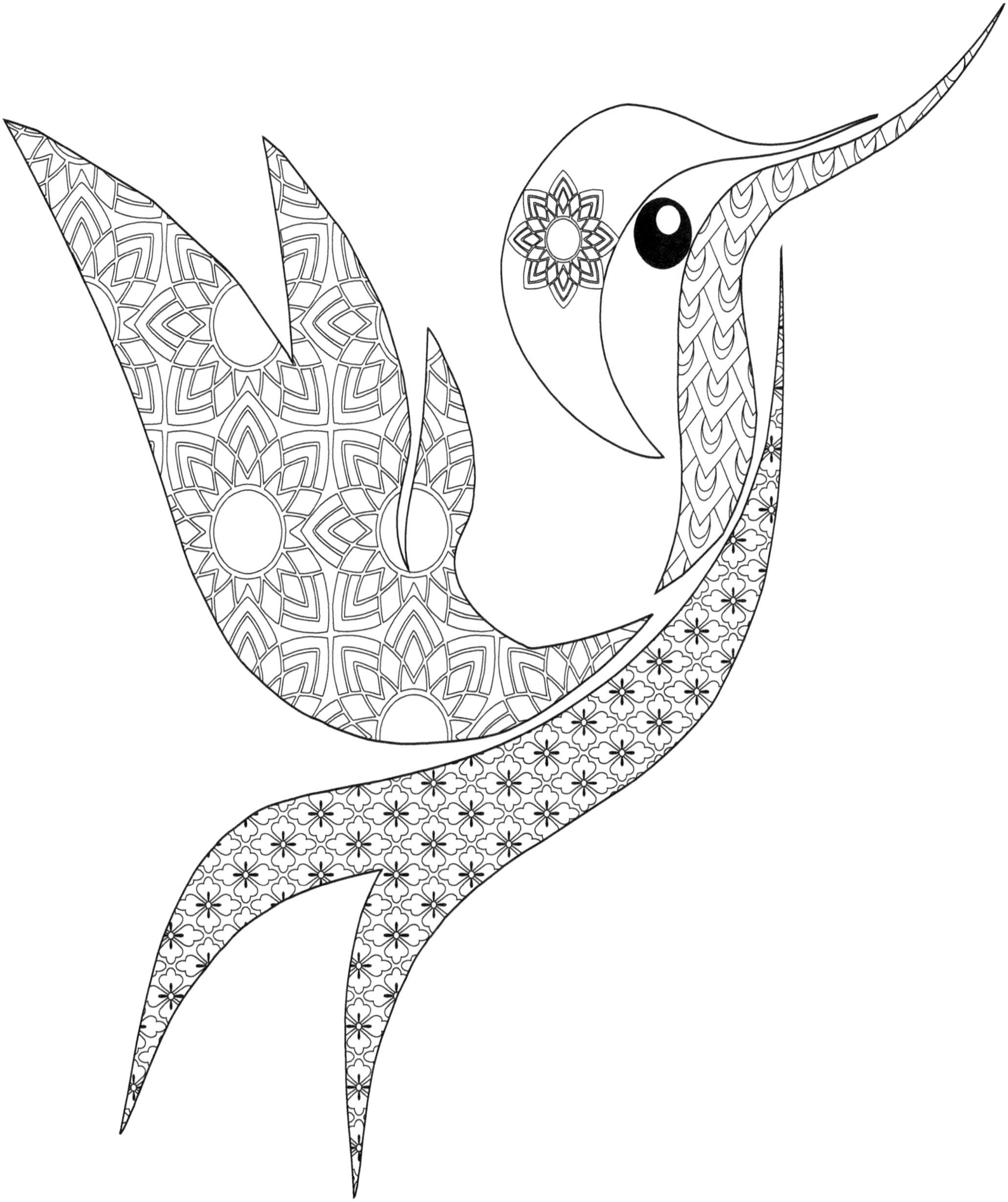

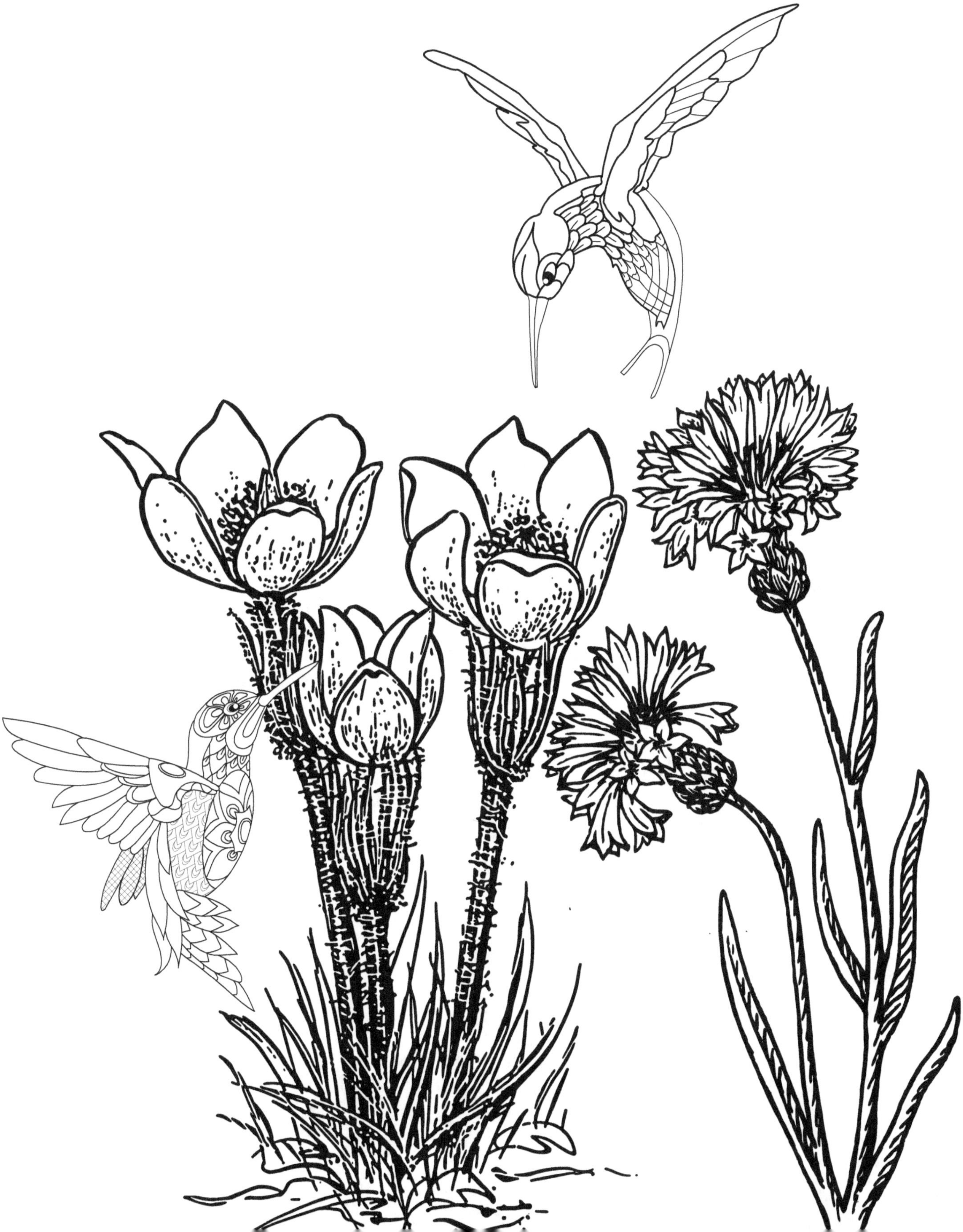

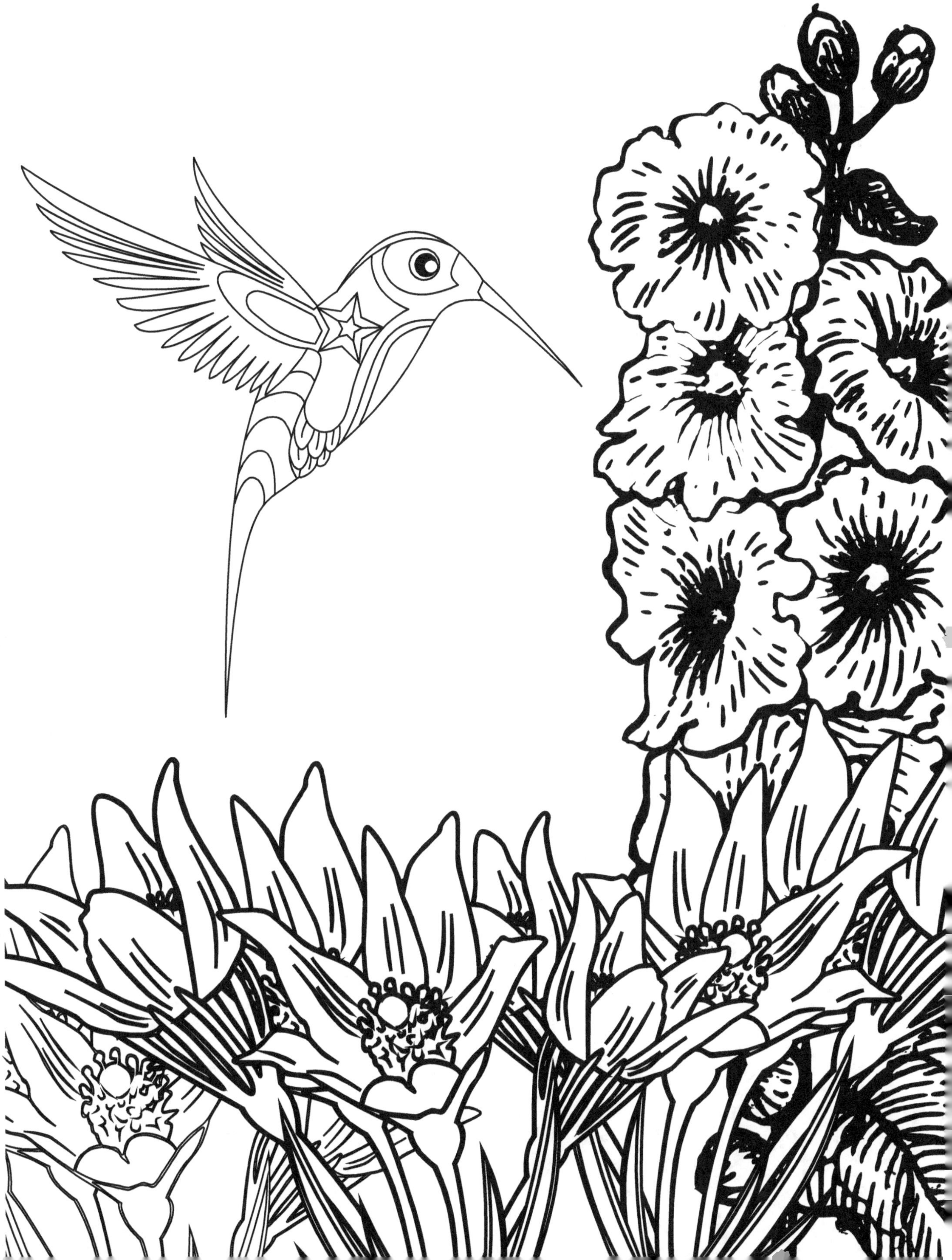

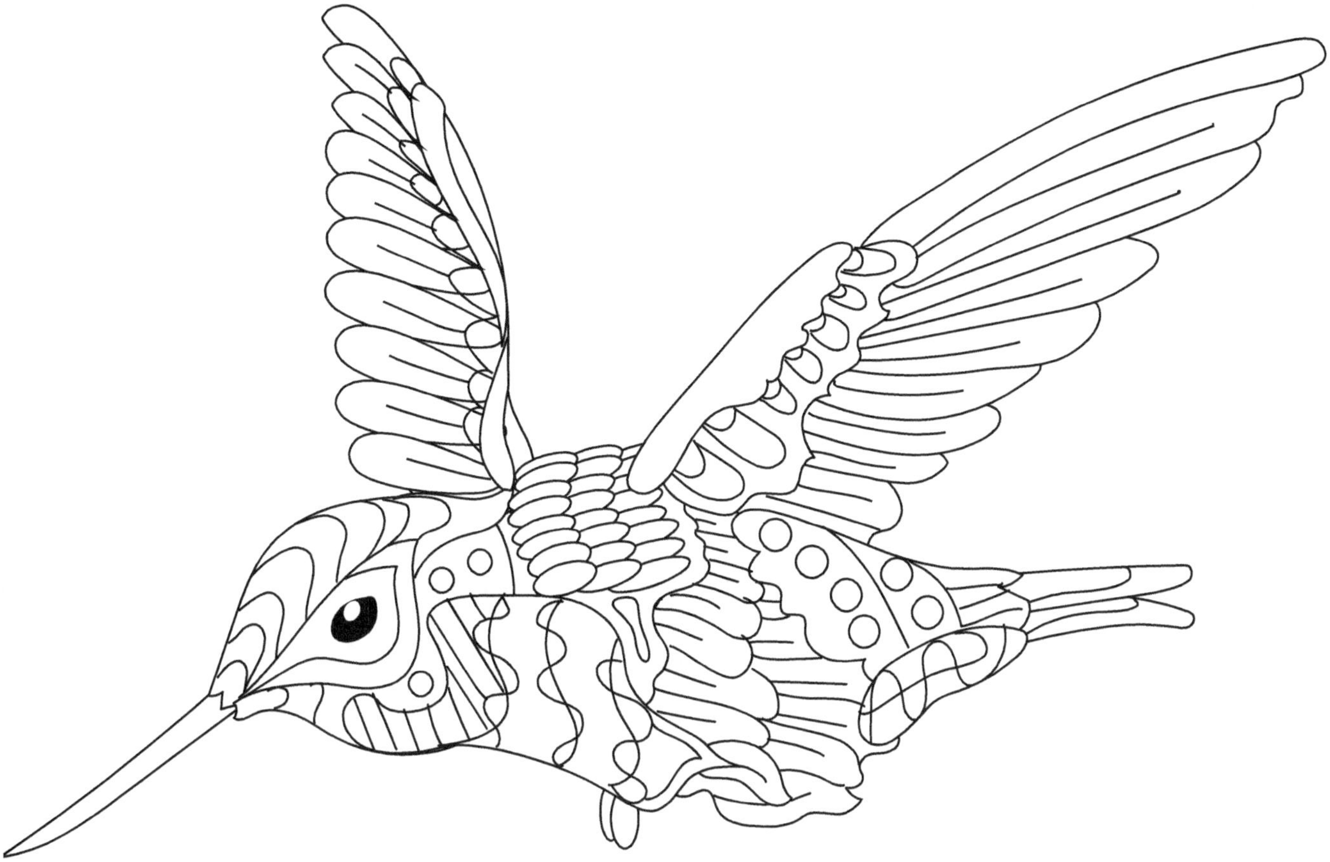

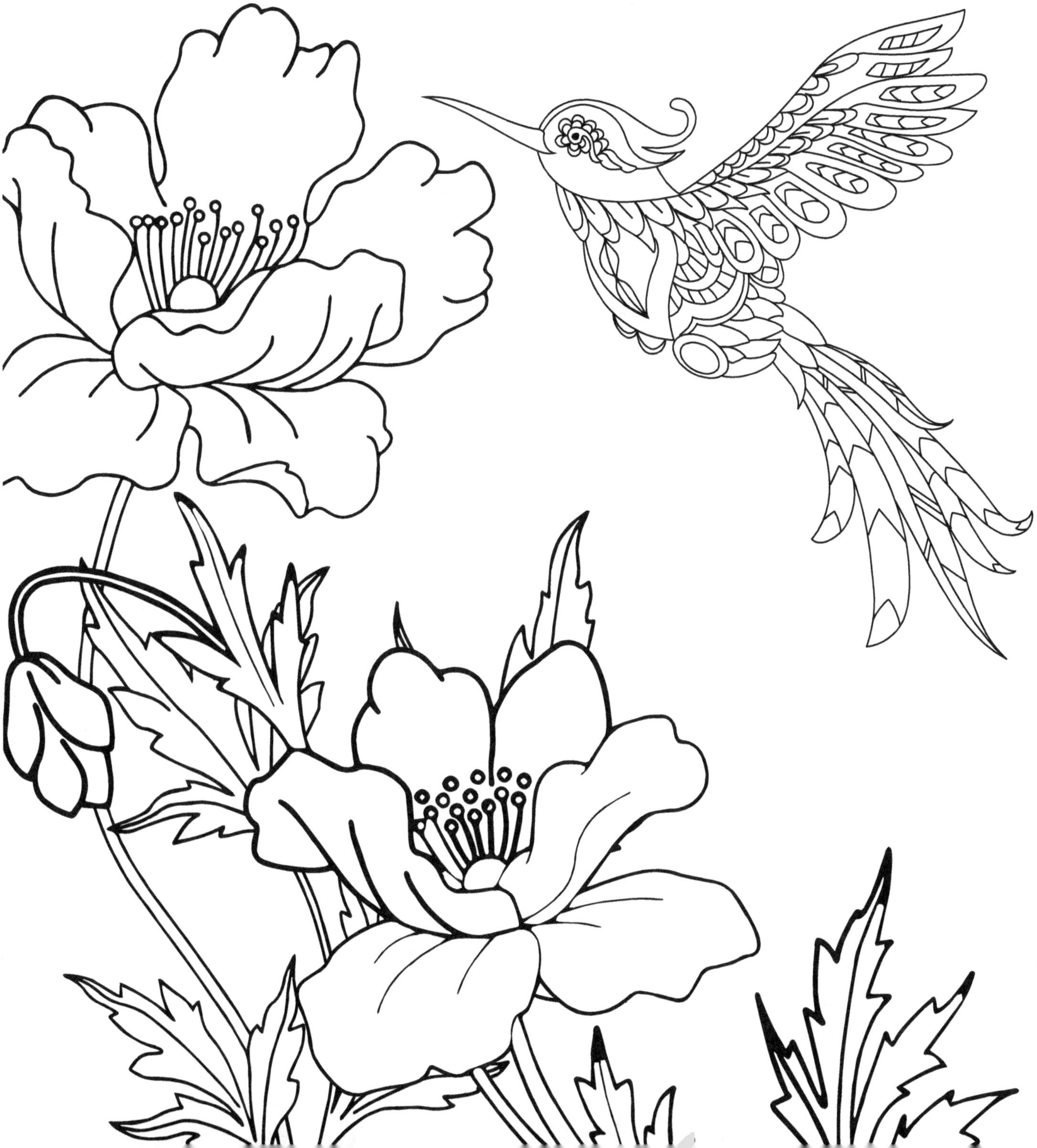

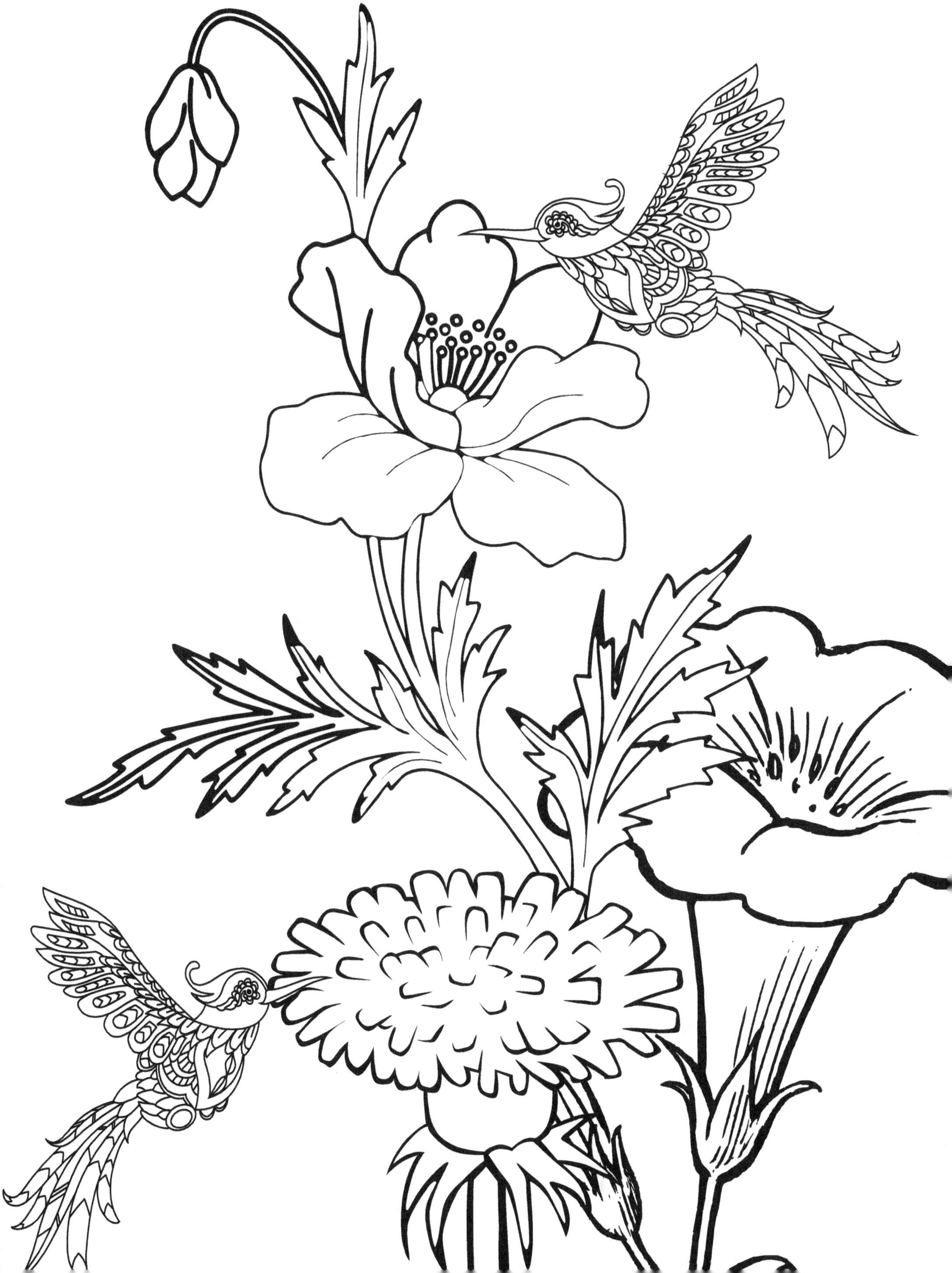

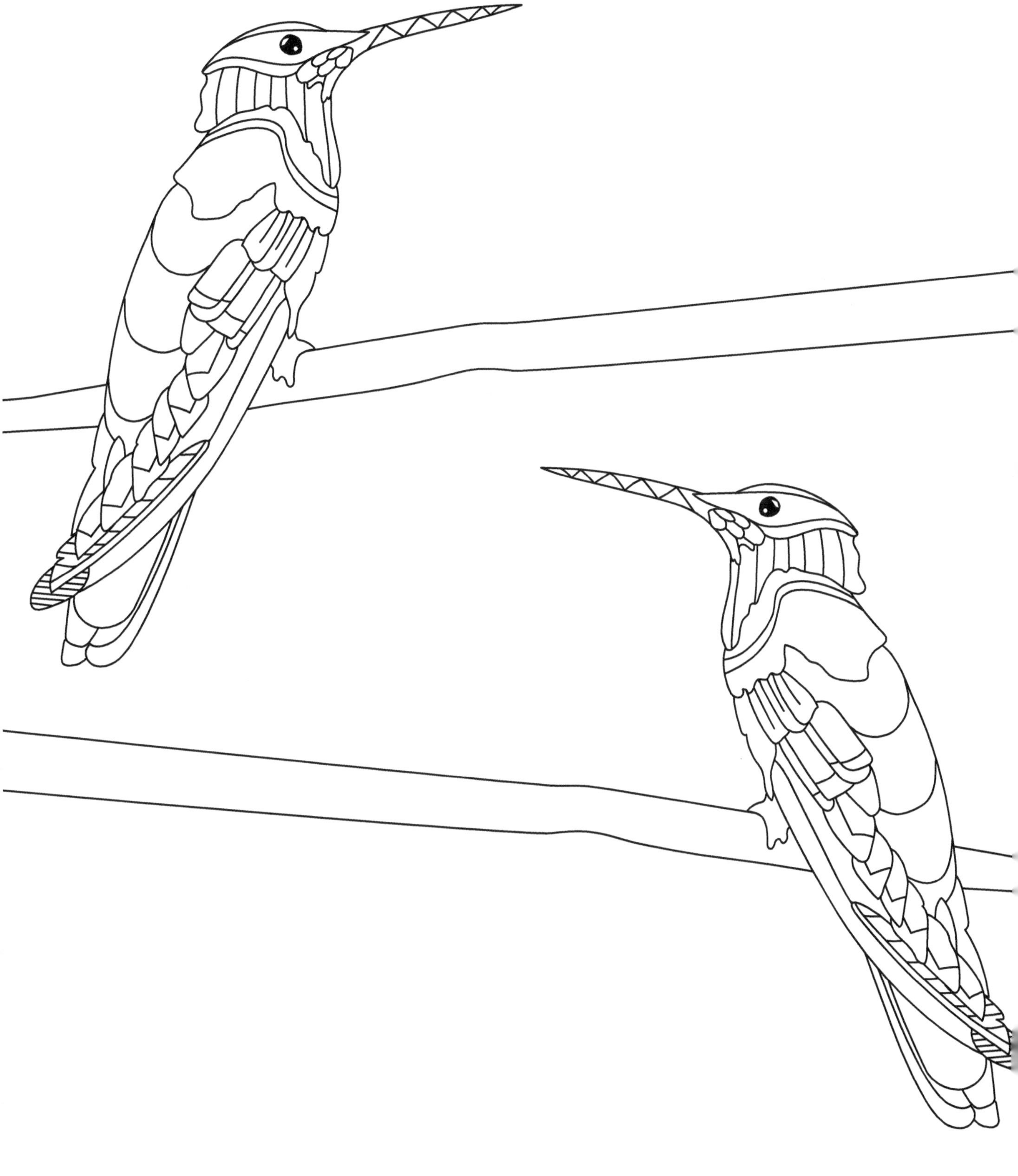

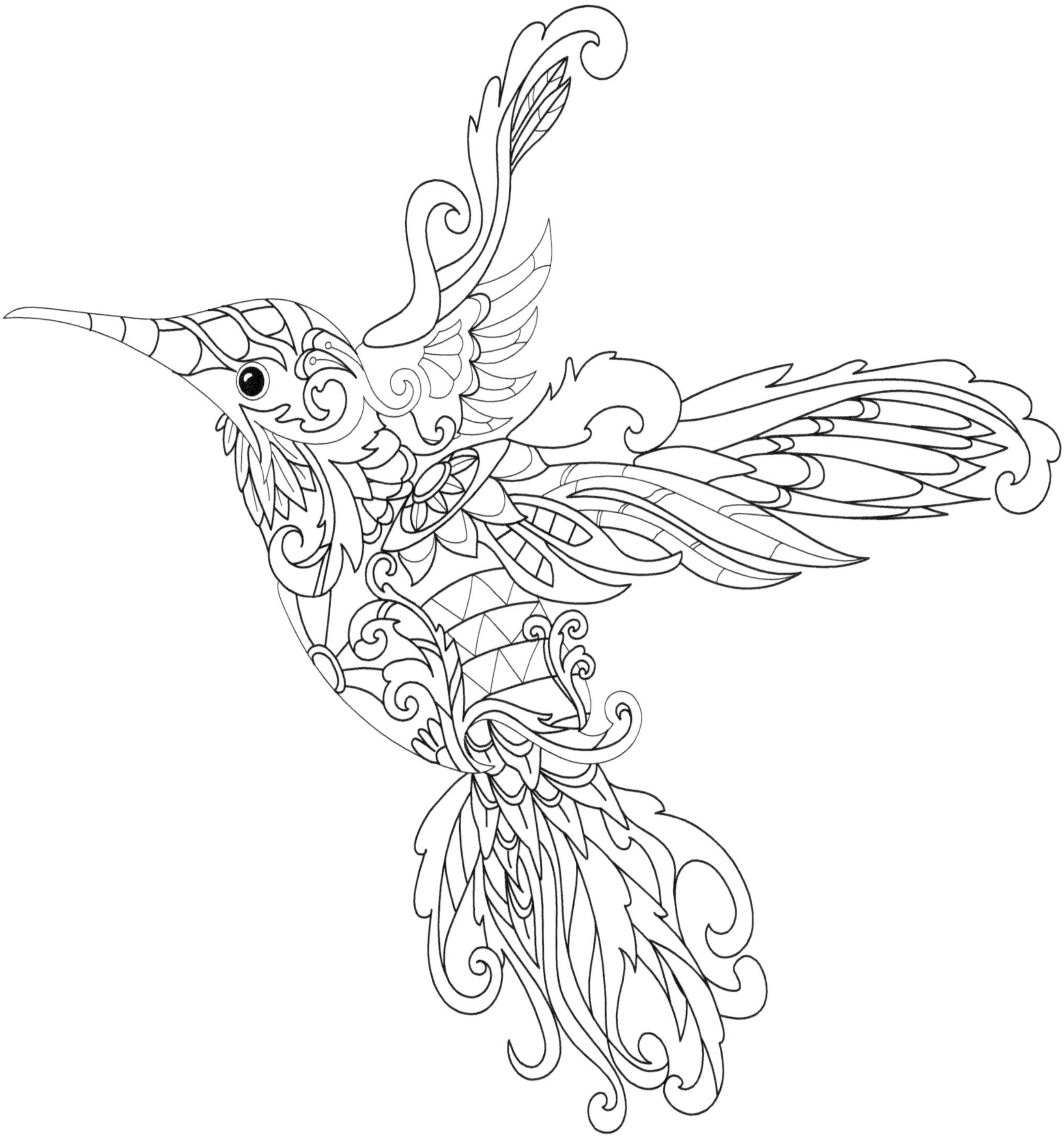

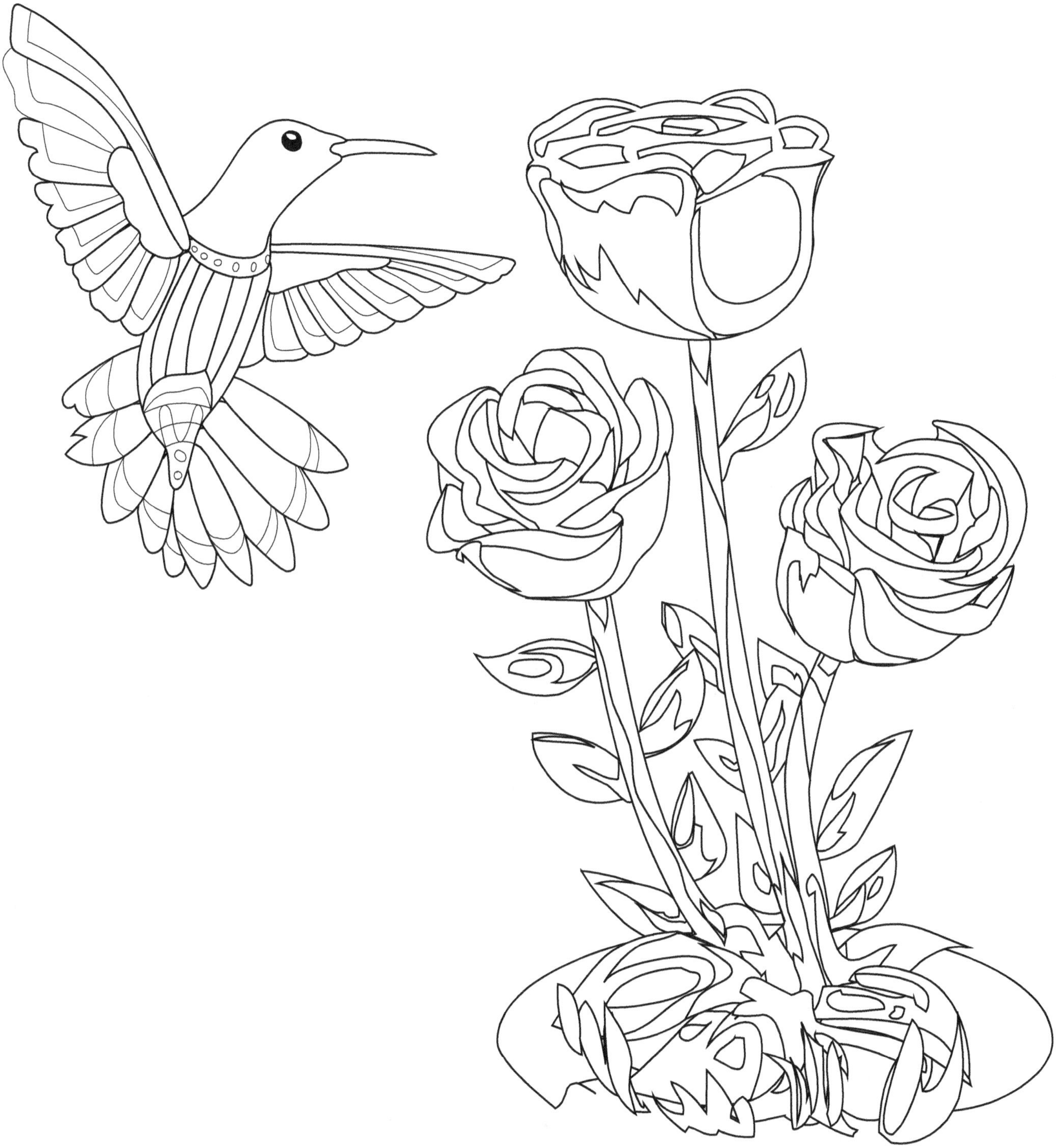

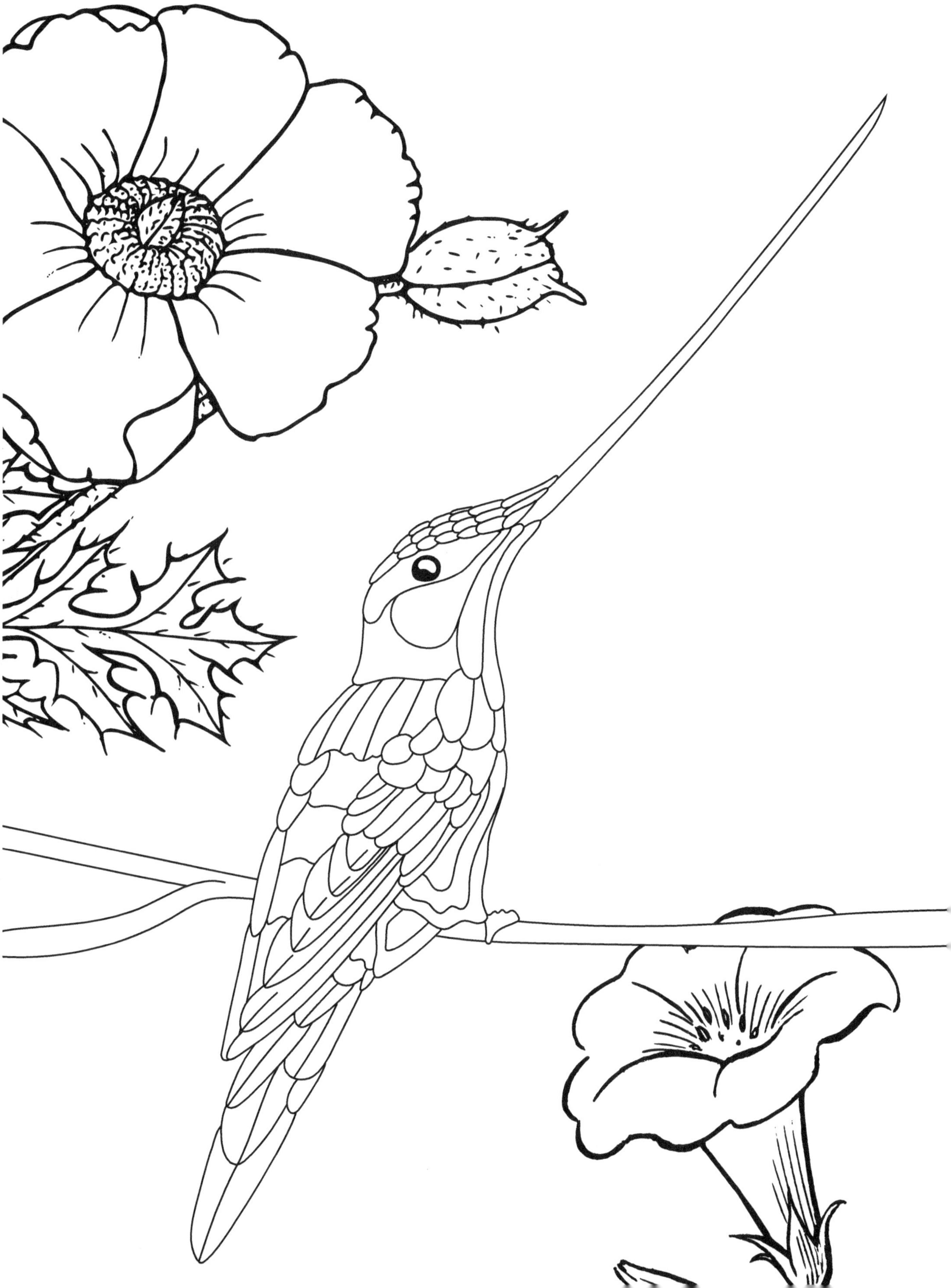

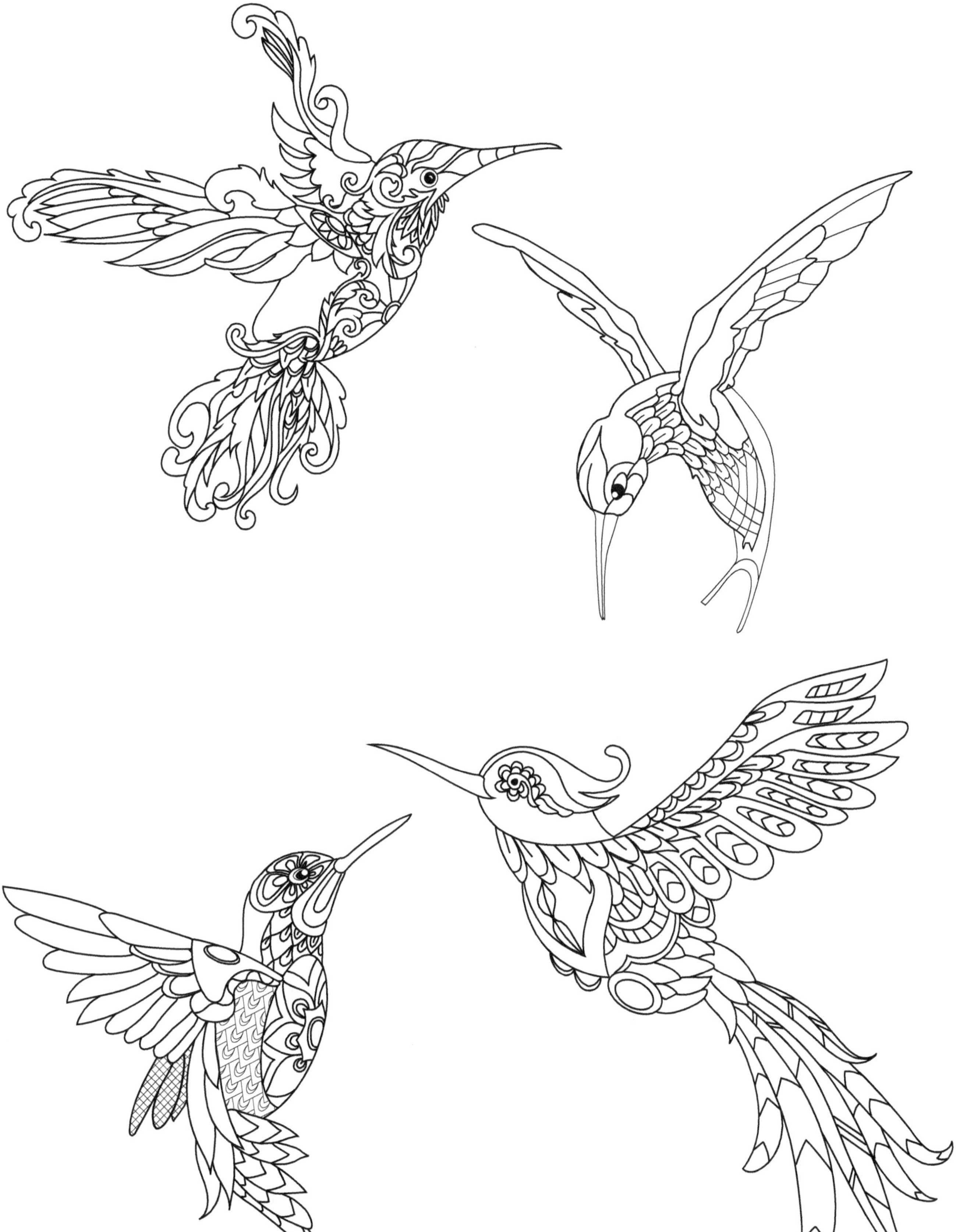

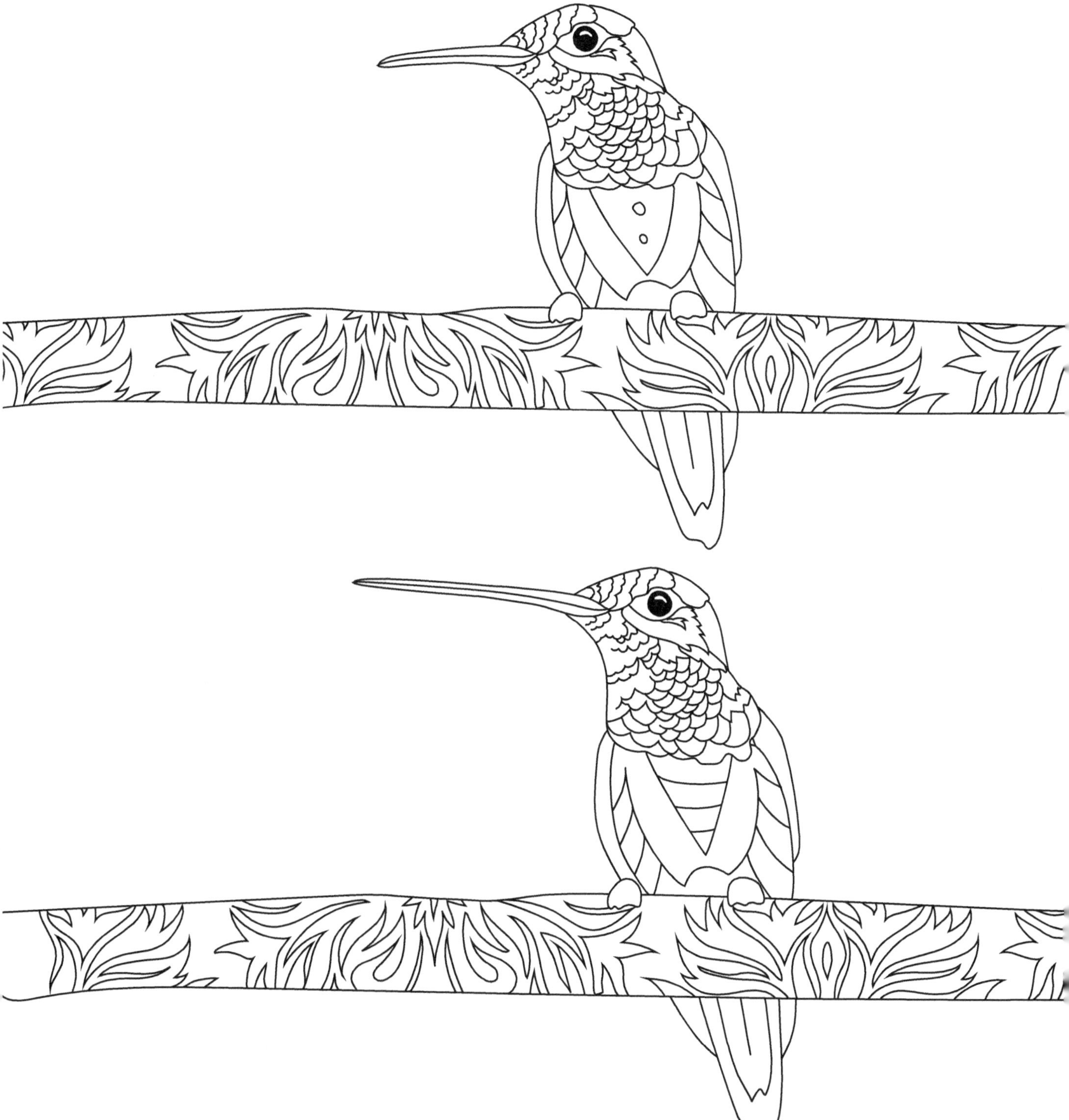

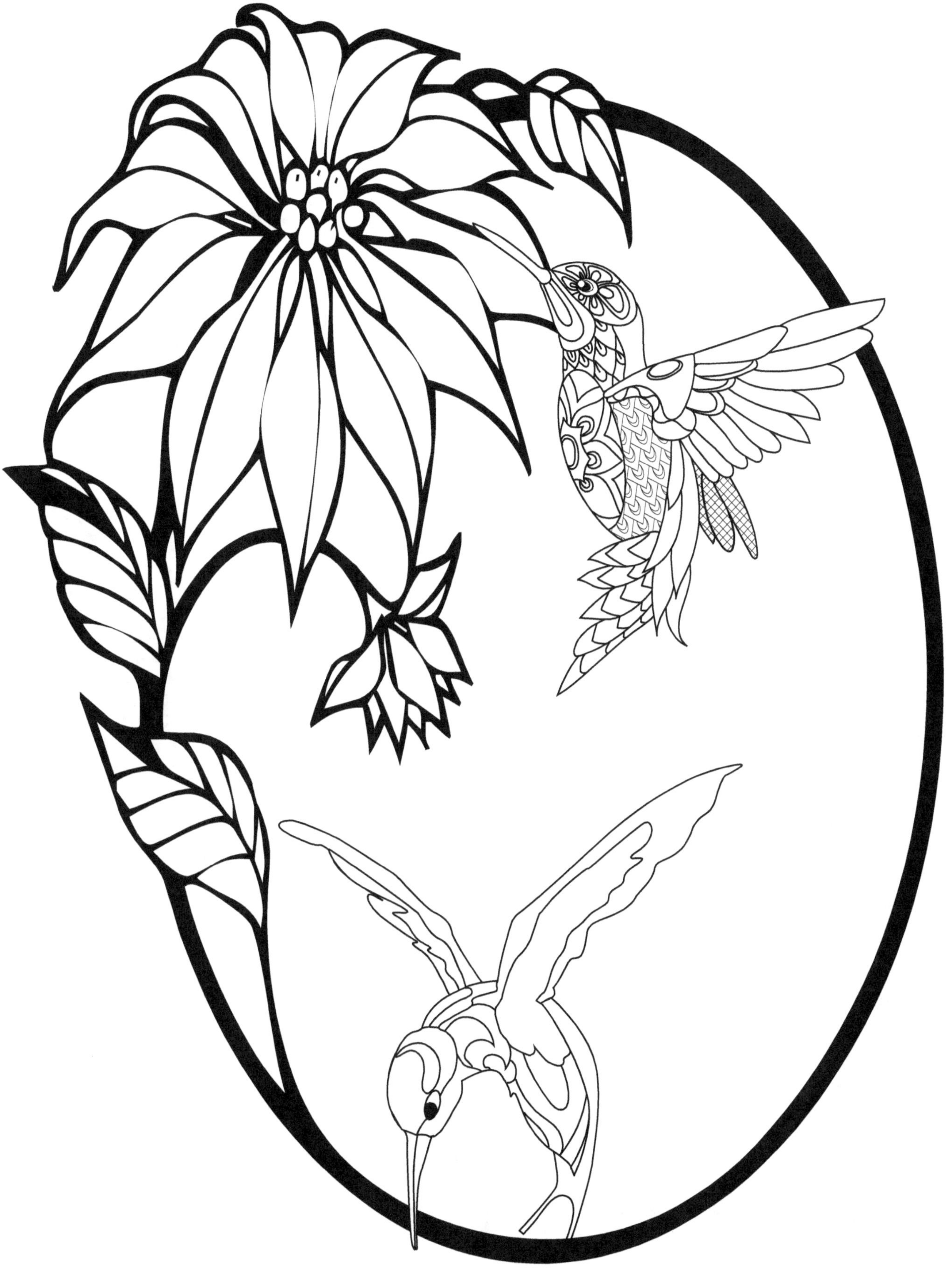

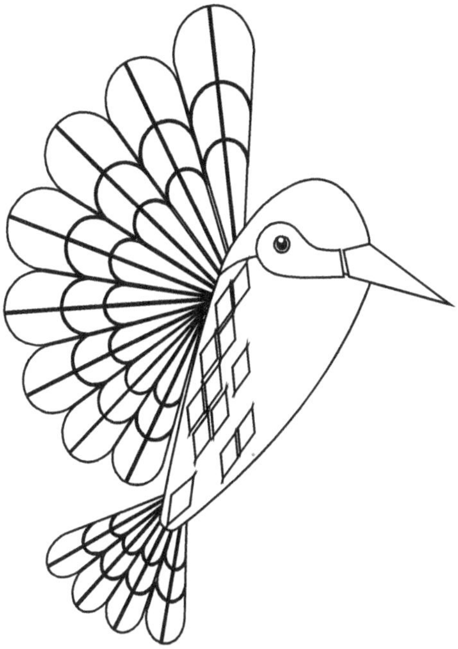
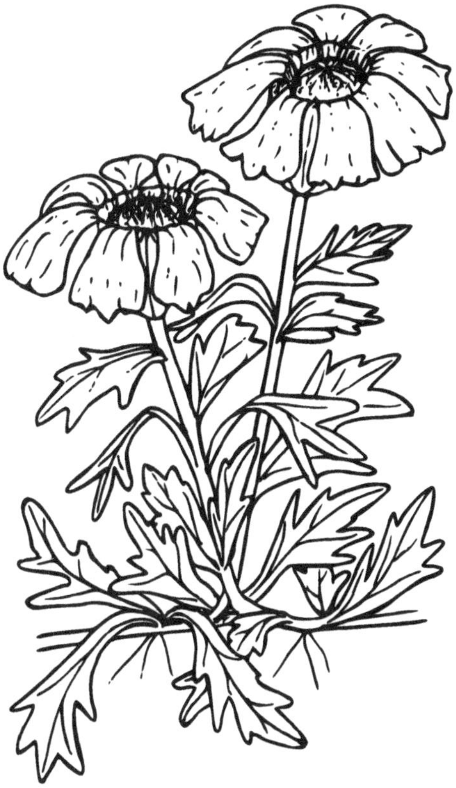
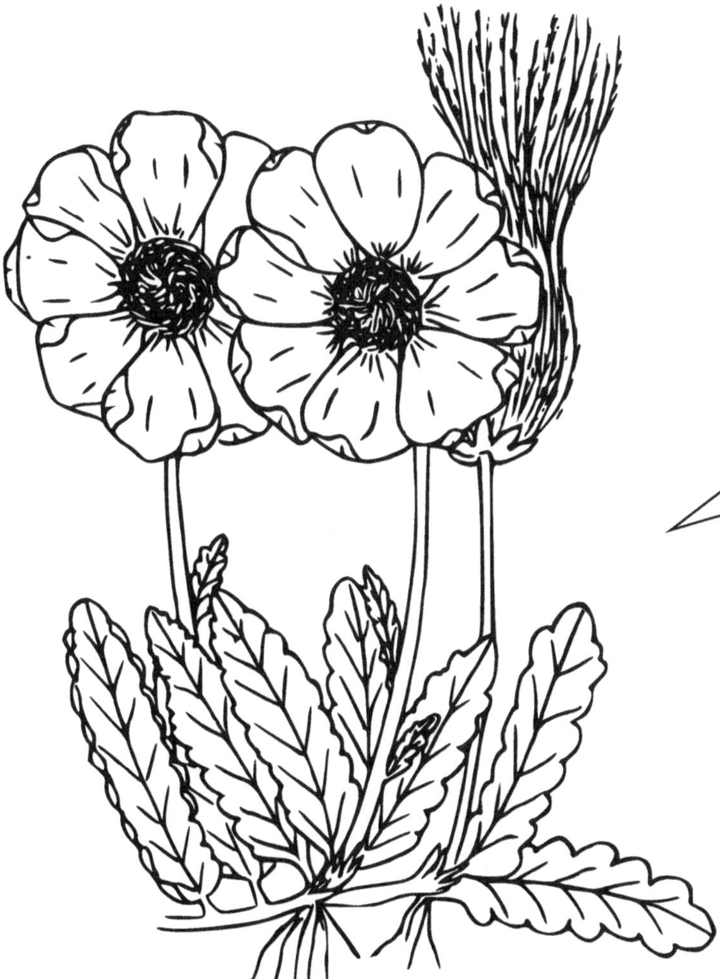
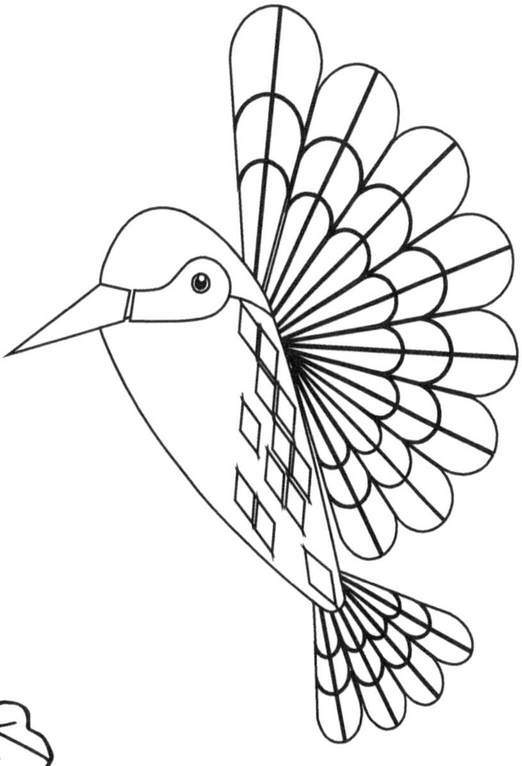

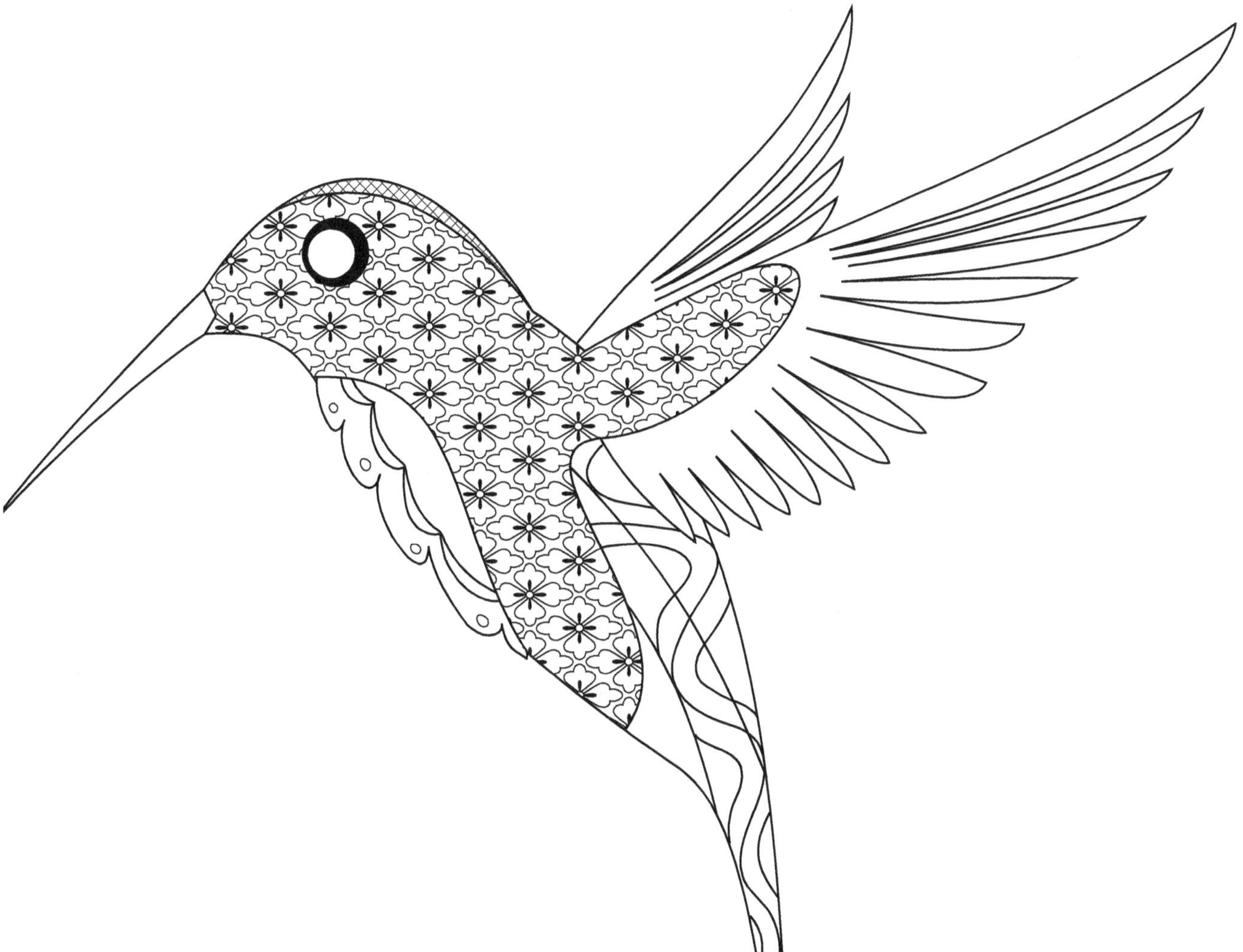

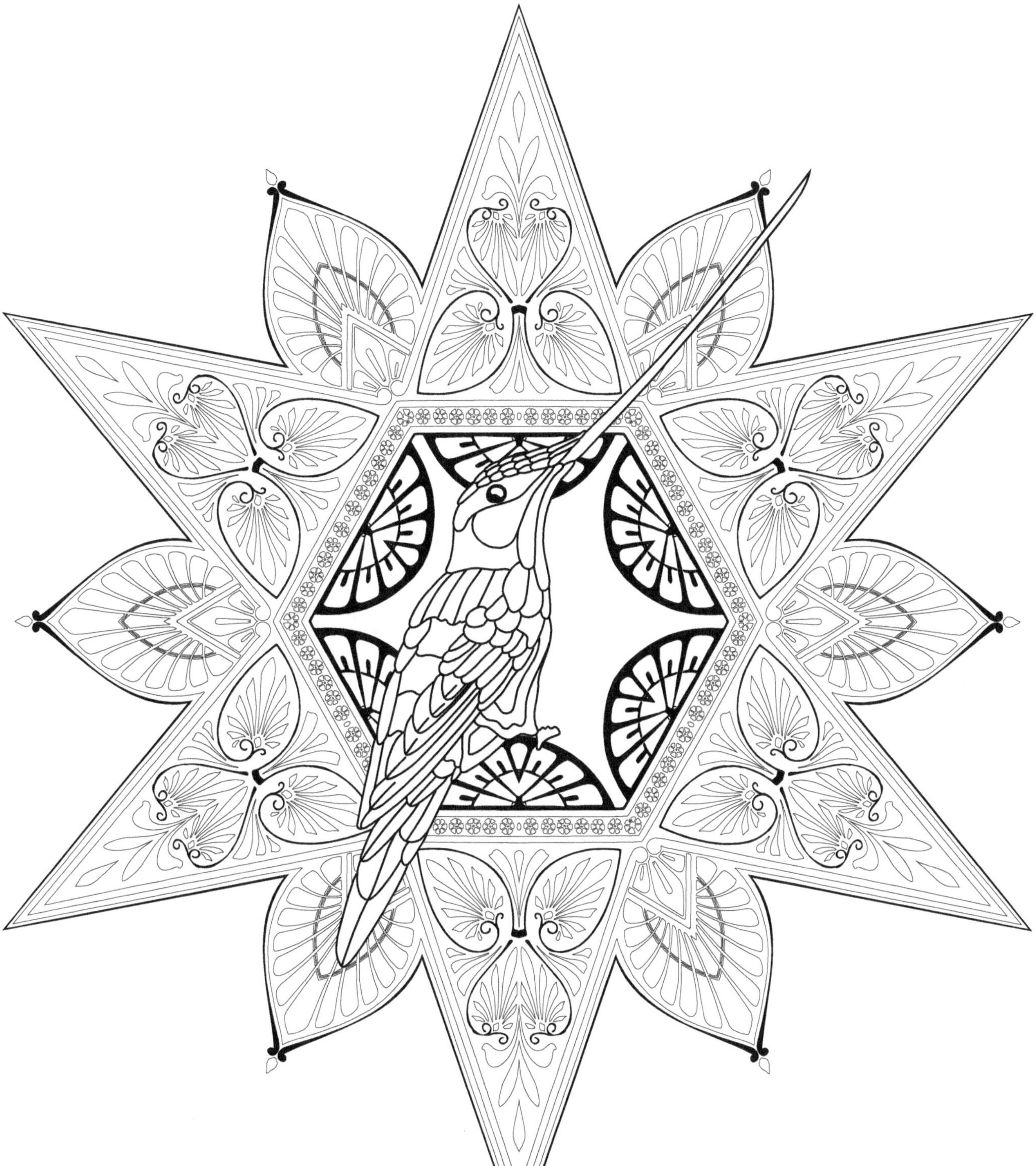

www.ingramcontent.com/pod-product-compliance
Lightning Source LLC
Chambersburg PA
CBHW060441220526
45465CB00008B/3230